SEX, STRENGTH AND THE SECRETS OF

BECOMING A MAN

A CELEBRATION OF SEXUALITY, RESPONSIBILITY AND THE CHRISTIAN YOUNG MAN

DR. DONALD M. JOY

Regal Books
A Division of Gospel Light
Ventura, California, U.S.A.

D0712026

Published by Regal Books
A Division of GL Publications
Ventura, California 93006
Printed in U.S.A.

Library of Congress Cataloging-in-Publication Data
Joy, Donald M.. (Donald Marvin), 1928-
    Sex, strength and the secrets of becoming a man : a celebration of sexuali-
ty, responsibility, and the Christian young man / Donald M. Joy.
    p.   cm.
    Summary: Offers guidance in life conduct and sexual ethics for Christian
teens, emphasizing the physical and emotional changes that accompany the
growth of adolescent boys.
    ISBN 0-8307-1392-1
    1. Teenage boys—United States—Juvenile literature. 2. Teenage boys—
United States—Conduct of life—Juvenile literature. 3. Teenage boys—United
States—Sexual behavior—Juvenile literature. 4. Adolescent psychology—Juvenile literature.
[1. Teenage boys. 2. Sexual ethics. 3. Conduct of life. 4. Christian life.] I. Title.
HQ797.J69 1990
305.23'5—dc20   90-44045
                                                                              CIP
                                                                               AC

1 2 3 4 5 6 7 8 9 10 / X3 / KP / 95 94 93 92 91 90

Rights for publishing this book in other languages are contracted by Gospel Literature International (GLINT) foundation. GLINT also provides technical help for the
adaptation, translation, and publishing of Bible study resources and books in
scores of languages worldwide. For further information, contact GLINT, Post
Office Box 488, Rosemead, California, 91770, U.S.A., or the publisher.

CONTENTS

Dedicated to four generations
of contemporary Joy men:

Celebrating Grandsons—
Justin
Jordan
Jason

Honoring Sons—
Michael
John

Accepting Myself—
Donald

Saluting Dad—
Marvin

Who taught me most of what I know
and now has shown me how to die.

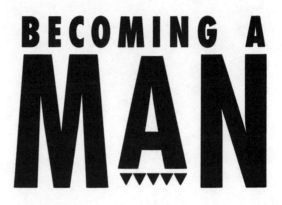

BECOMING A
MAN

CHAPTER ONE

SO LONG TO CHILDHOOD

WHEN you called to me the other day from the curb, Jason, I realized you are no longer a child. You are my peer—the same name, the same potential destiny—only a younger version of me. And Justin and Jordan are right behind you coming up into their manhood, too. Now and then I get to look at the video of your births—all three of you were delivered by Doctor Max Crocker. He held each boy upside down and suctioned your mouths before laying you in your mother's arms. I've heard my own sons choke up as their tears fogged the camera. Looking at the new "Joy" coming into the world was almost too much ecstasy to survive! I treasure my own Nikon color shots of each grandson taken during those early hours.

AWESOME

At a family camp in New York last summer I spotted a guy just hitting his teens. He made the U-turn in the cafeteria line and was facing me for the first time. He reminded me of you. So when this total stranger was within inches of sliding past me toward the food, I blurted out:

"Has anybody ever told you that you are dangerously good looking? And if you don't give it all to Jesus, you are in big trouble?"

He leaned close to me. I felt his breath in my face—this nearly six-foot tall 14-year-old: "There's this girl here that's been chasing me for two days saying she wants to date me!"

"See what I mean? You're in big trouble!"

MY PROMISE!

When I look at you, shooting up taller and filling out in your ultimate manhood, wrapped in boundless energy, I feel connected to the next century—through you. If you return the compliment, I suppose when you look at me with my marks of ripening age, you feel anchored in the past.

I am eager for your life to be full and rich and free. So I am going to set down here all of the "trade secrets" I know about being a man and living fully. My dad and my grandpa Joy did much the same for me. It is now more than a hundred years since my grandpa Charles Wesley Joy was born. He had never studied human growth and development, and did not have the advantage of great libraries and modern information centers. Yet my father and his father lived in transparent honesty with me. They never controlled me, but they did not hide their life secrets from me, either.

I am putting my best secrets in written words for you, first, because there are so many of them—too many for a speech. Second, I want you to be able to reread them, weigh them and decide what to do about the issues in your own life, without having to talk back to me. I respect you so much that I want you to sort and sift out the ideas. You have already shown me that you can make tough decisions and make them well. So I know that you will be able to shake down what is here, too, and to keep the parts that are true and right for all generations.

Some of what I am writing is very personal. Yet those secrets may be the most urgent ones for you. I have taught everything I am writing here, and some people have come back 20 years later to thank me for "being

I am eager for your life to be full and rich and free. So I am going to set down here all of the "trade secrets" I know about being a man and living fully.

there with the right stuff" when they needed it. After you've read my best secrets unveiled here for you, you can know that your grandmother Robbie and I are ready to talk with you any time about these or any other things that are important to you.

After I had unveiled a lot of my life secrets at a men's and boys' breakfast in Toronto a few years ago, the oldest man there—older than I am—slowly got to his feet when I offered to respond to questions.

"I have a question for you," he said. I thought I might have offended him.

"Where were you when I was 15?" he asked.

And in Texas, more than 10 years ago, a 13-year-old boy asked breathlessly after a similar breakfast talk, "Are you going to say all of this stuff to the women at lunch? I'm going to make my mom be here!"

Since most of my seminars and lectures are far from where you live, you are not likely to slip in where I am teaching. That's another reason I have written the urgent secrets here for you. You don't have to travel or pay a fee to hear me talk.

GROWTH!

Three years ago you asked at Chi Chi's Restaurant whether you could sit at the adult table and order with us. The other five grandkids would be ordering from the children's menu. We were four generations deep, and I welcomed you to the adult table. You wanted to order from the adult menu, even though you were in your last legal year for ordering from the kid's menu. But when you were still hungry after devouring the adult meal, I endorsed your dipping into the privileges of both worlds. So, you ordered a second "child's meal" to fill your hungry spot. Your sister, brother and cousins carried on like carefree children at their table nearby. But you had entered the world of adults. You listened, talked, laughed and participated in everything with the rest of the adults in your larger family.

FOR ALL YOUNG MEN

I am writing not only for you, but for all boys who are bursting through into their full manhood. You remind me of the urgent questions I had as I was hitting my teens. I am also writing this book for hundreds of young men who have backpacked with my students and me in our "discipleship development through trail camping" adventures in the Daniel Boone National Forest in nearly 20 trips since 1977. For all young men eager to embrace life and to achieve their highest dreams, I'm offering this book. Check the Table of Contents. You can begin anywhere and the stuff will make sense. I wrote it "straight through" mostly, so it may read best that way. But let your real questions dictate what you go searching for first. As these brief chapters unfold, I will be offering you the best information I have. Here are the issues and the chapter numbers:

1. *You're a priceless, precious, one-of-a-kind person!* In this chapter I have saluted you. I not only admire you in every way, but I think I would "lay down my life" to shield you from anything that could hurt you in any way.

Sexual energy can be harnessed and managed and released in wonderfully constructive ways.

2. *Putting the right foot forward.* You are walking into some heavy issues: "male identity," "male role" and "adult responsibility." And you are ready for all of them, so I will lay each one out so you can see it as if it were a mirror on your wall. You have everything you need to make it safely and well into full adult responsibility. But not all boys do, so I want your journey to be a blessing and not a tragedy. That is why I want to give you a "walking tour" through some of the choices. And that's why I will describe some of the feelings that come with the territory of your new manhood.

3. *How to examine your "roots" as you become your own person.* You will be making good choices about your future family and ways you will want to build quality into your own children's lives.

4. *Go for the gold!* Since some people around have other plans for you—wanting to use you or to drag you into very destructive things—I've provided some tips on how to set goals for being a responsible and trustworthy person.

5. *A picture of what you are and want to be.* This painting is true of every healthy boy as he embraces his new adult status. And since you are the prize of such males in the human species, I'm pretty confident I will hit the target. Give yourself permission to add notes in the margin about specifics that I don't know about.

6. Decisions, decisions, decisions—ideas on making the right choices. Some people worry that the biggest decisions anyone makes are those that come between 15 and 25. But I will be writing a license for you to wear the responsibility well, to use the clear imagination and reality base that you are already using and to go for it! If you can describe who you want to be and to become, and what you want to achieve, then I'll offer some strategies for turning those dreams into reality.

7. How to manage your male "hydraulic sex system." I am calling your sexual energy the "tiger in your tank." By that name, I am suggesting something about its high energy and its inescapable splendor, but also some of the risks to men of all ages who do not respect its power and keep it nicely under control. Your sexual energy can be harnessed and managed and released in wonderfully constructive ways.

The first thing Dr. Max Crocker said about you, preserved on your dad's videotape, is, "It's a boy!" And in between, the most important identification you have ever worn is your sexual identity. As you take responsibility for the domain of your manhood, I will tell you all I know about managing the "tiger in your tank" and rising to full responsibility and pleasure as a man.

8. How to survive through hard times. I wrote a chapter I hope you never need to read. I've called it "Coming Back When Things Go Wrong." On second thought, you may need to read it, because with your kind of open and honest face, somebody is going to confide their tragic story by telling it to you. The people who trust you enough to tell you the trouble they are in may be desperate enough to give up on everybody and even on life. So the chapter can be your "good news" for people who are in pain or trouble. And you need to know, yourself, what the bottom line is if you ever feel like giving up. Since you live, along with me, in a crazy world where terrorists, mad bombers and Pied Pipers of the worst sort are working the crowds, I have closed chapter 8 with the "bottom line." I will tell you where I stand with you if the going gets tough, or worse. I am for you—unconditionally!

9. *All the questions you thought nobody would ever let you ask—and what the Bible says.* Since you, like me, have found Jesus calling you to the best kind of life, I've put together a chapter that offers a walking tour of what the Bible has to say about sexual things. If anybody ever suggests to you that the Judeo-Christian Scriptures are "negative" about human sexuality or the vision of becoming fully alive and human, they haven't seen the material I've pulled together for you here. Grab your own Bible as you read chapter 9. You can locate anything I have quoted. Check out what comes before and after the parts that spoke personally to you or that made you really curious.

Justin, Jordan and Jason, I always belong to you, and you can always find me. For the benefit of other young men, I'll publish my phone number at the end of chapter 8—the chapter dealing with pain and trouble. I am eager to hear from anybody who needs encouragement to pick up the pieces and get on with the whole and healthy good life.

HANG ON!

So that's the promise and the list of issues. Take your time, and write your questions in the margins. This is a personal book beamed into your life at a time when you deserve the privacy of a locked room. It is information that opens life's best secrets, and gives you permission to ask all of your questions in a safe place and expect answers you can trust.

CHAPTER TWO

MAN, HOW YOU HAVE CHANGED!

GARY had looked forward to entering Marsden High School. It was the mark of growing up. The first-year students were a new mixture from three other middle schools, so he'd meet lots of new people.

The guys he had run around with at Ingalls School were "mall rats." They roamed their favorite mall an average of four hours each day, longer on weekends, and spent more money than he could afford at the video arcades. It cost Gary at least $20 a week just to hang out with them, and they often spent that much in one afternoon. There had been some shoplifting, just for kicks, and the mall security guards were aware that their little fraternity of guys was not always good news.

Gary made a decision. Looking into the mirror one Saturday afternoon as he was finally getting himself together for the weekend, Gary decided that he was handsome. *But,* he thought, *I'm sometimes a rotten person, and I don't like that.*

What he saw in the mirror as he was locked away in his parents' master bath for this luxury shower and general reflection time was this: *Here I am, taller than Dad and a lot better looking, thanks to Mom's side of the family. I'm lucky to have such a good body, but I didn't have anything to do with getting it. My hair is just like I would have ordered, and my eyes, too. I wouldn't have changed anything.*

Gary told me how thankful he was, as he said, "Just born to be me." I heard a similar story from Steve, who was adopted. He once told me the same thing. Steve saw that he was a foot taller than his dad, and very different in every way from his mother. "So," this adopted 14-year-old said, "I just stood there looking at what was happening to me, and really liked what I saw. I had this awesome year-round tan (something other guys envied). And my biceps looked great without even pumping iron or anything! Then I got tears in my eyes. I had sometimes felt sorry that I was not really my parents' natural kid. But Dad weighed about 110 and was only a little over five feet tall. And here I stood at six-three. So I made this little prayer: 'God,' I said, 'whoever those folks were who gave me my genes, bless them and tell them I said thanks.'"

FANTASTIC GENES

Steve and Gary had not always cared much about their glorious genes. Before they hit full height, there had been the carefree years when they didn't even know they had bodies. Combing the hair, brushing the teeth and taking baths were frustrating details parents demanded. But such chores wasted precious time; they were stupid things that made no sense.

Somewhere around age 11 or so, the world began to look different. Their blue jeans got too tight and too short. Shirt sleeves in the winter didn't fit right. Gary's hair texture actually changed. He had shining, straight hair that he had just begun to comb and to notice during seventh grade. Then as his shoe size began to jump suddenly, his hair literally kinked. He used bunches of mousse to try to make it lie straight, and to shine, but it waved! It took him a while to realize that the sharpest guys in the world were spending money to get hair like his.

And Steve felt a little ashamed that he didn't "look" like a Carter. His parents had always told him how special he was and that the day they got him at three months was the best day of their lives. But he looked so different from them. When he was in fourth grade he was almost as tall as

Puberty refers to the biological changes that mark your transition from child to adult. You literally get a new body, a new look.

his dad and that seemed odd. There were about two years of acne—pimples all over his face and shoulders. That was no fun, and he felt like the "great speckled bird" out of the folklore.

But both Gary and Steve were settling into their new, manly bodies with a lot of pleasure now. At 15, fully grown, Steve confided to his grandma, who always gave him clothes for special days, "This is the first Christmas that I can think about increasing my wardrobe. Always before, I've had to have new things just to keep in basic clothes. But I haven't outgrown anything in a year, and it's going to be fun to add the things I really want this year."

PUBESCENCE AND ADOLESCENCE

So, exactly what's going on; why does your world suddenly seem so different? You're growing up! Pubescence and adolescence have hit.

Puberty refers to the biological changes that mark your transition from child to adult. You literally get a new body, a new look, new hair scattered all over in very adult places, and the arrival of your fertility—your sexual ripening. "Pubescence" is a word built on the term "puberty," which refers to a two-year period extending from the time you began your wonderful growth spurt and transformation from child to adult, up through the time you gain your full height and are sexually ripened—capable of adult reproduction. Everybody knows that pubescence has ended when you develop hair on your face that matches the color of your hair. "Fuzz" only announces that maturity is on its way. The color has to go in before you're a man.

"Adolescence" is something else. Adolescence refers to the gap between the time when you are fully grown and biologically mature, and the time that the whole world respects you as the adult you knew you already were. So "adolescence" is something your culture creates—like a prison from the end of pubescence until you are allowed to embrace your responsible manhood: Enter the work force, marry and take responsibility for a family of your own and for your own career.

Behold the Face!

About the time you discover your face in the mirror and begin to suspect that other people are staring at you, you develop skin blemishes. Acne, pimples, "zits," are the curse of growing up for many people. Your whole body is a chemical laboratory exploding during pubescence. Sometimes you will wish you could put a mask on that says, "Closed for Renovation"! During pubescence you'll often feel like you are caught in a disaster zone. But look at it this way: *It is worth waiting to get this new improved body.* So talk to yourself in the mirror and thank God for the changes. You will like the finished product, even though there may be some days when you think you don't look so good. The chemical side effects that show up in skin blemishes are actually signals that your whole body is being transformed. If you like the idea of becoming a man, with all of the rights and responsibilities that go with it, then celebrate the pubescence problems.

Choose your soap carefully. The young male body often needs two very different kinds of cleansing agents. You need a skin care soap to keep the acne under control. But you need a powerful deodorant soap to keep your

"Adolescence" is something culture creates—like a prison from the end of pubescence until you are allowed to embrace your responsible manhood.

armpits and body from smelling like walking death. All deodorant soaps are very harsh. So a bath may seem like a two-tone paint job. You need delicate skin care for the face and shoulders, but war zone treatment from there to the knees. And if you develop tender feet, athlete's foot or a thousand other problems inside your shoes, you need the tender skin treatment for the ankles and feet, too. Take heart! When pubescence and acne season is past, you can make a few seasonal adjustments to keep your skin comfortable and smell good year round without all the fuss.

Watch your teeth, too. By now most of your "baby teeth" are gone. You may even get "wisdom teeth" behind your heavy duty molars by the time you finish high school. A few guys do. Or they may have to come out. That is no fun, but most of us don't have much luck keeping them. Check the straightness and evenness of your teeth and the alignment job where they bite together. Your dentist can coach you on how to brush to keep them clean without damaging the thin porcelain coating that you will want to last a lifetime. If you have overcrowding or otherwise crooked teeth, this is the time of life to get them fixed. An orthodontist can work miracles, even with an adult with irregular teeth. But the early teen years are the very best. The "Closed for Renovation" sign is one that a lot of teens wear during these school years while they get their teeth lined up.

Use some common sense, though, and see if you can develop some habits that would correct mouth structure and straighten teeth. If you were to spend an hour a day, for example, playing a horn with a large, circular mouth-piece, you could straighten most irregular alignment problems. So if you ever thought of playing an instrument, start with a trombone, baritone or tuba. The large circular mouthpieces of these instruments press against your entire dental area. At the same time, you are pushing with air pressure behind the teeth. The combination is just right to reshape your mouth into the best of all dental displays! And you will learn how to read music, how to play with an impressive group and the dental work comes free. Your gums are very flexible during your teen years and can be reshaped easily.

HEIGHT, HANDS, FEET AND HAIR

The human body is an amazing collection of matched parts. Your feet, for example, are an excellent predictor for your height. Occasionally there is an exception, but the longer the shoe size in early teen years, the taller the man is going to be. And the rule about when you are "full grown" is this: You will keep growing taller until your hair color-matched beard grows bristled and feels like sandpaper within 24 hours after shaving it.

You probably have discovered that the distance from fingertip to fingertip, with your arms spread out against a wall is exactly your height. So, if you are six feet tall, it will be exactly three feet from the tip of your fingers on either hand to the tip of your nose, facing straight ahead.

Boys turning into men develop patches of hair under arms and in the groin, and a hair cover over legs, arms and chest—to varying degrees, of course. Boys having Asian or American Indian genes tend not to become as hairy as those from European or African descent. And the "hairy monster" is more likely to go bald by mid-life than the less hairy-bodied man. You can count on one thing: The whole combination of genes and good grooming will turn you into the gracious, handsome and good person most needed on this planet now. So speak to the mirror again and thank God for what you see: "I'd rather be me than anybody else who ever lived!"

TRAIN TO WIN—NOW!

When the idea hits you and the opportunity comes, jump into training for lifelong skills. You'll be richly rewarded today—and tomorrow! Here are some of the stakes worth going for.

Team events. If you choose contact sports, here's what you'll gain: an opportunity to build your body and watch your diet, as well as a chance to run with the right crowd—guys who are committed to excellence in training and who are learning to play and win by the rules. If the coaching staff at your school does not have this kind of integrity reputation, think twice, because you could be robbed of some valuable benefits. If you are serious about discipline and excellence, consider community or volunteer leagues that have the top reputation for developing positive people.

In all team events, you are building physical skills as well as social skills. "Team players" tend to be very productive in adult careers of all kinds, and they tend to take people seriously. That makes for good performance anywhere.

Don't overlook other team opportunities that may be more your style: debate, drama, orchestra, band and choir. These are less rigorous in physical training than contact sports, but they often require intense mental skill development, a sense of rhythm and tonal precision. The benefits are lifelong, and may continue as recreation and practice well beyond the adult days of tough football. Music and speech skills, for example, tend to last for a lifetime. And any group-event skill may eventually turn you into a coach, a minister or a director—and your career spans much of your lifetime.

Individual events. Jump at the chance to compete against yourself. Train for piano, triathalon, cross-country, golf, tennis, vocalist, skiing, skating, swimming—whatever. Work on stretching yourself and becoming the best you can be. While you may be part of a "team" for some of these in major events, the discipline is mostly individual, and your competition is against the clock or the judge's pencil. You are pressing for excellence in a field where you are fully responsible for the outcome.

The benefits of individual events are mostly personal. You have a sense of who you really are, what you can do and how far you can go. You may turn pro and carry on to an adult career after the Olympic competition you dream of. And when you scan the list, you will see that these are activities which you can enjoy for a lifetime, even if you do not turn professional and make your career out of your youth training and skills.

I am urging you to get involved for two reasons. If you are ever good at any of these activities, you must start young. More importantly, you have incredible energy and tons more time now that will be harder to find when you grow up. Many guys hit college and wish they could play the piano or a guitar or the drums, for example, but the hours of training are much harder to chip out of a college day. So, get started now while you're in elementary, middle or high school.

Welcome to the world of your manhood! I am eager to help you and your family virtually abolish the "prison" of adolescence. You are ready to be taken seriously as a man. Now! Stretch to the new responsibilities that come to you as a young man, and give your parents a chance to trust you with more and more responsibility. It looks good on you!

CHAPTER THREE

CHECK THOSE ROOTS!

HOW does he manage to always be here?" You were watching as your dad rolled up in the family car at a four o'clock junior varsity event. The other man with him, it turned out, was a business contact from out of state. The hour and a half before dinner with the guest brought both of them to the sidelines to watch you and your team.

Your parents were always there for you. When your report card in fifth grade suggested, "Can do better work!" your mother had some questions: "Is that true? Could you do better?"

"Well, maybe," you replied, "if I didn't do anything but study. But I have it figured this way: I'm going to college, so I need to save some of my brain until I get there. I don't want to use it all up now."

Your brain theory was wrong, of course, but you provided a winning entry in the Joy family book of humor.

"HIGH INVESTMENT" PARENTS

Jason, you were lucky to have parents who had their eye on your future. They figured out who you were and what your gifts were. They found ways of working with your best motivations—mostly by doing things with you when you were little. That is how you learned to love to work: Doing it with Mom or Dad was fun! So today you are loving your school work and your contact sports, and you manage to volunteer at the emergency room. Work is fun! That means your whole adult career is going to feel like a game. You will sometimes want to apologize to your employer for paying you—you enjoy everything you do as if it were recreation. Boys who have only a single parent can get double responsibility and share the work. This often helps them capture their true manhood ahead of schedule.

High Value Son

From the very start, you knew your parents were going to show you the ropes and teach you all they could. They had no secrets when you had questions. Somewhere about age 10, you knew you were getting big chunks of responsibility. You could do almost anything that had to be done around the house. Your mother had worked with you so that you could have survived, even then, if they had been flat in bed suddenly sick. You could manage the whole house. Everything out-of-doors was familiar to you. Only driving the car was off limits. But with your careful training on lawn equipment, even the car was only inches away from your skills.

You answered the phone knowing exactly what to tell people who were trying to reach one of your parents. Sometimes, when the caller stated the problem, you knew what your dad or mom would say, and you offered the information.

When you goofed, nobody panicked. Whichever parent was on hand would simply keep you focused on your own future, and say, "What do you wish you had done instead?"

You exploded a few times, angry at your parents but mostly at the feeling that your own independent future was so far away. Even then, your parents wouldn't fight with you. They could have, because you were temporarily pretty rotten to them. But they had their eye on your future and knew that dealing with anger was a lifelong responsi-

The "Intimate Family" places a high value on everybody in the house. Everyone knows he or she is free to choose. So they have to be good choices—choices with consequences that are easy to live with.

bility. So they offered you options, asked questions and finally said, "You choose. Take your time. Whatever you are feeling is OK, but it is not OK to treat people like garbage. So cool down, then tell us what decision you have made among the options we've all brainstormed."

I've been describing here the "Intimate Family," which places a high value on everybody in the house. And in that family every member has more and more responsibilities. Everyone knows he or she is free to choose. Those choices will affect other members of the family, so they have to be good choices—choices with consequences that are easy to live with.

Some boys grow up in "Competing Families," in which there is always tension over who decides, who gets the best stuff, and who controls everybody else.

Others live in "Chaotic Families," where nobody seems to care whether anybody had basic needs met or has a

future of any kind—it's every kid and parent for themselves!

Even more guys live in "Showcase Families" where the
stress is on "looking good" to outsiders, and that can make
a lot of stress. In these families, one person makes almost
all decisions and also decides what looks "showcase."
That can keep you pretty tense, and lead to some dishonesty with true feelings. It's common for kids to feel "used"
in order to make the family "look good."

Intimate families, in contrast, don't need to be embar-
rassed about anybody in the family. Everybody is valued,
and the family's reputation is really in everybody's hands.
This means that the risk of living with the consequences of
their choices is a risk everybody knows is worth taking.
There is a high investment in teaching the children everything they need to know, and everything about the parents' beliefs, values and decisions. So nobody worries
about occasional poor decisions, because they can be
remedied some way.

MAXIMUM MOTHER

You were really a lucky fellow. You knew long before I
could describe it that your parents and your family are
your "First Curriculum" for growing up healthy and secure
as an adult.

A boy needs about 15 years of consistent mothering
by a good woman who provides warmth, discipline,
praise and a lot of "sounding board" feedback. If his
mother doesn't meet these needs, he is often hurt or at
least underdeveloped in some predictable ways. But
with a healthy relationship and plenty of mother-pres-
ence, you will find that you automatically have these
gifts:

- You easily trust other people in basic friendships and social contact.
- You can express complicated feelings, and are ready to join and make commitments to community, church and in marriage.
- You will feel confident in your own developing masculinity, which has blossomed under the affirmation your mother gave you as she tutored you in how to do and to say the right and masculine things.
- You will have a realistic and healthy view of the sort of young woman who would make a solid lifelong partner.

You have been lucky, for sure. Many boys get a lot more criticism than affirmation from their parents. When Mom isn't able to give good discipline and feedback to a boy, most boys know to look someplace else for mother-affirmation. Often this comes from a teacher, a youth leader at church or a coach. Some guys I've met actually hooked up with a buddy who had a healthy and available mother and sort of adopted her to get the basic, minimum supply of positive mothering they missed at home. Others, even as adults, have "adopted" or borrowed a "Mom," as they often call her, simply to charge the batteries that almost went dead during childhood and the young manhood years.

Boys make good survivors, though, and tend to find some safe "mother" somewhere if theirs turns negative, or disappears. Some boys actually marry a woman who will mother them. It can work, of course, but that often leaves them without the "bone of my bone, flesh of my flesh" partner that a wife and lover needs to become.

FANTASTIC FATHER

Boys desperately need their fathers at a couple of points in their journey from conception to launching out on their own. From birth to about six years old, boys "rehearse" their masculinity and manhood behaviors, and imitate their fathers down to ridiculous details. Dads "teach" masculinity in the years from birth to about age 10. Then, mothers "polish" their sons' masculinity or sex role, as rehearsal

> ## When Mom isn't able to give good discipline and feedback to a boy, most boys know to look someplace else for mother-affirmation. Often this comes from a teacher, a youth leader at church or a coach.

directors, from about age 10 until they are launched as responsible, loving husbands.

Eventually every lucky boy has a father to rescue him from his mother and to set him free—believing he can make it as an adult male. Mothers are more likely to "hang on to their baby" too long, so this is the second special gift most boys get from their dads: the confidence that they can take responsibility to eventually get launched, and to be "on their own."

Here, again, if a boy misses his father, or if Dad is too busy, gone to much, is an alcoholic or is otherwise caught up in his own problems or his career, the boy can suffer seriously in those first six years and at launching. But boys who make up their minds to learn everything they can about the adult world of a responsible male will automatically pick the "model" men outside the home. They hang around with a friend whose dad makes a priority of being a father to his son. Or they get involved in scouts, church clubs, symphony or summer athletics and check out a safe and continuing "father surrogate" to imitate. Since there are very few men teaching in kindergarten or elementary school, it is sometimes hard to find good men unless you are in those volunteer programs at church, summer recreation or community clubs.

Boys who have healthy, available fathers who contribute to a stable, consistent childhood with discipline, affirmation and a feeling of safety tend to be able to do these things:

• They can make moral judgments based on what is fair, what protects their own and other people's rights.

• They find it easy to believe in God—in the unity and order of the universe.

• They can adopt rigorous self-discipline to achieve goals they choose—even if it means saving, waiting or "going against the flow" to get popular approval.

• They have a consistent game plan for how to treat a woman well, how to envision marriage and how to resolve conflicts in the family.

It would be easy to imagine that either a mother or a father could get you ready for all of life. But mothers do their work almost without noticing the ways they are making their contribution to you. And fathers usually do their work naturally, too. If either of them needs to "be a parent for the other parent" or "do the whole parenting job alone," it tends to come with a lot of work. So you were lucky, indeed, to have both parents doing their spontaneous parenting with you. To show you how "easily" they do their work, let me tell you some things that happened to you very early.

Moms and Dads Together

If anybody had seen your actual birth delivery, they would have seen you held tightly in your mother's arms very soon. Mothers "encompass" their babies (hold them tightly to their bodies) the same way everywhere in the world. Fathers simply cannot hold a baby in that same way for very long, but mothers do it instinctively. Mothers do that encircling embrace in a way that looks like magic. Mothers keep doing this "encompasser" if they can.

There is a famous marble sculpture done by Michelangelo called *The Pieta*. It shows Mary holding the dead body of the adult Jesus as He is taken down from the Cross. Michelangelo sculpted Mary in the cuddling, rocking position, holding her adult Son as if He were still her baby. Mothers stop holding you like that by the time you are six or eight years old, but their "encompassing" love still surrounds you in much the same way their arms once did. Robert Munsch has captured this "encompassing" mother image in the amazing children's story book titled *Love You Forever*.

What your dad did for you was a very different thing. Dads hold the baby out in front of them to look in the little guy's eyes. As the baby gets more strength, fathers hold their babies at arm's length, move them up and down and all around—always "face-to-face" and always doing these wonderful games with them. This is called "engrossing" behavior. You can see why dads are more likely to finally say, "My son is ready to go away to college," or "Our boy can make it on his own. Look at the good decisions he has been making since he was 10." Dads have been rehearsing this separateness, this "autonomy" from their child's birth. Dad's ease of separation has been shown as early as the day of birth—simply by the way he holds the baby.

In an equally opposite way, your mom helped you to develop relationships, to "attach," to value other people. But your dad is more concerned with integrity, honesty, justice and fairness. He can sniff out deception or dishonesty in people and protect you from their exploitation. The best moral development research shows these differing centers of value: relationships for women and justice for men. So you need healthy doses of both father and mother experiences.

SUPER SISTERS

Boys are lucky to have sisters. Hold on a second—it's true. It doesn't always seem lucky, but it is—REALLY! Boys who have sisters as well as a mother know better how to deal with women. And if you are in a healthy family, you know that girls are as important as boys, and that they deserve freedom, responsibility and trust just as you do.

If you had an older sister, you likely got an extra dose of "mothering" from her. That's OK, because if you had a younger sister, you likely did your part in "fathering" her. It is not uncommon for a brother-sister relationship to feel a little like "parent to child" or "child to parent." But sisters, whether older or younger, are "other." So you will remember times when there was a tremendous advantage to having a sister, and at other times she was like an outsider, an intruder.

Women and girls think and work in ways that baffle us. So you will have had good practice in dealing with "the female perspective" if you were able to handle the brother-sister relationship without either of you going crazy. Sisters are different from mothers. Mothers know they are responsible for us and they build bridges of understanding to us. Sisters rarely take the time to be so kind to us.

BODACIOUS BROTHERS

When your younger brother was born, Jason, he chose Saturday morning. I think it took about six months for you to forgive him for taking you away from your favorite TV cartoons! But I have watched you two now for a lot of years. You are doing some "fathering" things for him, of course, since he needs a mentor and teacher. You mastered chess, and coached him until he became the third place national chess champion in his division! As a teacher, I know the feeling! Nothing is more rewarding than to see your "student" go further than you had a chance to go.

The two of you have developed a deep bond that only brothers share. At times, he's your best buddy. You "understand" each other in a way that would make it easy to "conspire" with him. At other times, he seems like your worst nightmare. When there is conflict, you will likely mount a stiffer battle because you are both "wired" as males. Your sense of justice/fairness, and the obligation to be "right"—even to use "power" to make your point—sets off a very different dynamic between brothers than is typical between a brother and a sister.

In families where each child is valued the same and where everybody is learning all of the secrets of managing the house, the meals and the whole show inside and out, brothers can be very different. One can be an athlete and the other a musician, and everybody can be healthy and know everybody else supports him. In the showcase, chaotic or competing household, however, ugly things can go on between brothers. Often one of the boys becomes the family "scapegoat." If that happens, he is the victim who catches ridicule, shame and sarcasm. This kind of family life tells us the whole family is sick, and needs help.

Bible stories of Cain and Abel, and Jacob and Esau, remind us of tragic things that can happen between brothers in conflict. Usually such families today need outside help—a pastor, a doctor or a counselor—to get their eyes on the really important things: the real worth everyone has in God's view, and the importance of keeping present problems focused on solutions that buy the future and try to guarantee a healthy adult life for every child.

FAMILY

Dad and Mom, of course, are models and referees at the same time. So the health in your family tells us that they have shown all of you how to be responsible men and women, and that you are all good learners. But they have provided ground rules to protect everybody in the same way. No sarcasm, no violence, "talk-it-out" and "tell-your-feelings" strategies have given you a lot of strength as a new man.

All families have conflicts and tears, and every member of a family will sometime be violated by others in the family. But you have been lucky to be under the roof of a family that has kept its pain "up to date" and has not allowed anyone to suffer day after day. This has been a wonderful gift from your family, Jason. And you are wearing it beautifully. The two words to describe that gift are "security" and "responsibility." The next chapter is a celebration of those gifts.

CHAPTER FOUR

DREAMS DO COME TRUE!

WILL I die? I want to grow up to be a daddy!"

I was listening to a boy who is now "a daddy." He was only five years old and was trying to get off to kindergarten. I was busy putting a temporary bandage on his wrist after the storm door banged shut in a high wind as he was leaving to board the school bus with his brother. There I was, trying to decide whether to take him to the emergency room for a professional butterfly bandage or to do it myself and take him to school. But I was also fighting back laughter. What does a five-year-old know about "growing up to be a daddy"?

He was serious, and he had obviously set that goal of being a daddy as his life dream. What it meant was that he had figured out, in five years, who he was. That little five-year-old boy was himself as a male child growing up with a supreme purpose—to be a daddy. It was a powerful compliment to me—his daddy. And it was a wonderful compliment to his mother. Being a daddy requires a "mommie," too. Here was our young son fixing his vision on a specific, visible image for the future.

At 19, home from college for the summer, that same boy, now a young man, presided over the final hours of the life of a cat he had enjoyed for a dozen years. After burying the cat he returned to ask me if I wanted to see the grave. This fully grown man had not only buried his well-tended cat, but had gathered the late fall flowers from the garden and decorated the grave. There was more. Here was a text printed on a piece of plywood as a tribute to a special cat:

> **Here lies Tom Joy.**
> **He is no longer with us**
> **But we will hold him**
> **In our hearts!**
> **Died: August 28, 1975**

Both of us were wiping our eyes. I hugged that daddy-aspiring son of ours and told him, "I'm glad to see how much you care about Tom. I'm glad you have a capacity to love. All of this tells me that you will make a wonderful father. With that much love for Tom, you will always value people in your life."

HERE'S YOUR LICENSE TO DREAM

Whenever I replay my memory tape of that "I want to grow up to be a daddy" episode, I realize just how much my son taught me the power of a boy's early vision of his own life goal. So I want to give you permission to reflect, to imagine yourself being the person you most want to become and doing the things you most admire in an adult male. Here are some questions to put you in touch with your imagination. Go ahead and give yourself permission to be aware of your deepest longings and dreams.

1. *Add 10 years to your age now.* Imagine that you are on stage before a large crowd of people. What are you doing, with the whole world watching? When the hazy fog of your teen years lifts, what is the lifelong image you have of yourself?

2. Who are the people you see on stage with you in your 10-year vision? How did they get into your imagination? What is their relationship to you in the picture you see?

EVERY GUY'S VISION

It has always been true: healthy young men always have their eye on the future. On the day the Christian movement was launched, the words showed up in the inauguration speech recorded in Acts 2:14-21: "Your young men will see visions!"

There is one vision, especially, that young men consistently see. This is especially true of Christian young men, but it is also true of those who may not hunger for faith in God. The same vision shows up in children from poverty and from wealth. Every boy who has not been abused or abandoned has the same dream: *Somewhere there is a woman with whom I can share all of my secrets for the remainder of my life.* I call this the "exclusive, lifelong intimacy dream."

TAKE YOUR FEELINGS SERIOUSLY

I have known for all of my adult life that healthy and religious boys grow up with that "exclusive, lifelong intimacy vision," the "one-woman-forever" dream. But Robert Coles and Geoffrey Stokes reported on their research with 1,025 teens in *Rolling Stone* magazine subscriber homes. They found the same dream driving even the nonreligious teen males.

The Coles and Stokes research also found that teen guys fall apart more easily than teen girls when a relationship ends. Why? It all relates to the collapse of that "exclusive, lifelong vision." Boys, it turns out, believe that the first love will be the *only* love of a lifetime. "Casual dating" or "dating around" is evidently not what healthy young men want. You see, guys and girls are created for commitment and intimacy. This is why males are able to make profoundly deep lifelong commitments and to make them early. This is also why it hurts so bad when a relationship ends. It really is serious business. Young men who want to grow up and fulfill their hopes and desires need to take their feelings seriously. They need to work through the grief and loss before jumping into another relationship. "Blessed are those who grieve, for they will be healed of their loss" is an important footnote for men who want to rebuild their dream after a loss.

Going for Your Dream

If you have a pretty clear vision of who you are becoming and what kind of person your ideal woman will be, then you will take time to build the dream deliberately and well. Here are some things that have always been true about building an "exclusive, lifelong, intimate relationship."

1. *Intimacy—becoming really close to another person—is a "harvest" of patient months and years of getting acquainted.* Know the person well *as a person.* If you want a lifelong marriage, check her out to see who she is, where she came from on her family tree and whether she is healthy, happy and decent with everybody. True intimacy always grows slowly out of the solid soil of "knowing" each other casually and intently. All of the great Bible stories about loving couples speaks about "knowing" as better than mere loving.

This means dozens, perhaps hundreds, of hours watching and listening as the one you've got your eye on moves within the same group you do. Marriages fail at alarming rates when, before getting married, the partners try to become physically intimate—to have sex—without "knowing" each other well before the sexual fires are ignited. They may quickly kiss and touch or even be sexual, but they are creating a "bubble," not a solid, intimate relationship that's real and that will last.

Guys and girls are created for commitment and intimacy. This is why males are able to make profoundly deep lifelong commitments and to make them early.

2. Intentionally keep your developing relationship out in public. This ensures that "knowledge" accumulates well ahead of "intimacy." Intimacy is the goal, the payoff; and it is the cement of a powerful "lifelong, exclusive marriage." But premature intimacy or *pseudo intimacy* almost always explodes, leaving two victims with wounds that often haunt their marriages later. So if you are living in pursuit of that vision of yours, be sure that you are "getting to know" the girl *as a person*. Don't complicate the relationship by going too far, too soon.

3. Keep your relationship under family visibility. This keeps your "real-world time" in sync with your "intimacy-world time." From about age 15 on, your intimacy hunger may be ready to beat the calendar and grab the "woman of your dreams" right now. And with the energy and time you can muster, you could develop a fully ripened relationship and be ready for marriage in a year or two. What this tells you is that biologically you are healthy, and that you have a high priority for intimacy.

But the real world calendar of going to school, getting a job and just plain growing up—physically and emotionally—may be running a little behind your biological and intimacy calendar. Be candid with your parents if your two calendars are badly out of sync. They may be able to endorse an earlier "real world" calendar than you imagined. But for most of us, the only way to synchronize those two calendars is to contract with each other and with our families to guarantee that the relationship has no absolute privacy. Count on it; no one is immune from this rule: absolute privacy leads to premature intimacy! Watch out!

4. *Your maturity is being shaped as you take responsibility for the relationship. This is your most important life lesson.* The pleasures of intimacy are so strong and so appealing that they test your responsibility like no other life experience. Are you made of the right stuff? Will you pass the test? Here's what's at stake:

- Your honesty.
- Your ability to postpone going all the way too soon.
- Your willingness to take full emotional responsibility for your partner.
- Your readiness to take full legal and public responsibility for your relationship.

You will not be surprised to read everywhere that the divorce rate of couples who lived together and later married runs more than double the divorce rate of those who keep full responsibility and full intimacy locked together in a public marriage. It could be that something was lost by the premature sexual intimacy. But it is more likely that there is a lack of trust—a deep character flaw. It eats like leprosy in their relationship. Couples who lived together did not take full public and legal responsibility for each other, so they evidently fear that their partner will abandon them now or later.

Beyond this lack of trust, there is another problem with having sex before marriage. Everyone develops an "appetite" for sexual intimacy, and it is powerfully shaped by the first sexual experience. People who develop their appetite for intimacy without being responsible and without being committed to their partner are in dangerous waters. In fact, they're vulnerable to looking for nothing more than recreational sex. They have an appetite for sex with a partner for whom they need to take no responsibility. Their appetite for sexual pleasure is shaped to want "sex for fun" with somebody, somewhere who doesn't also have to be a partner in paying bills, raising kids and being responsible for a thousand little things every day of their lives.

But couples who share their "responsibility" and their "intimacy" forge a bond in the crucible of "real-world" experience. These are the people who find that they are excellent lovers not only when they are on vacation, but day by day, in the middle of meeting payments, working long hours, sitting up with sick children and facing the whole agenda of real life.

So go for your dream! Check her out, of course. But really get to know her—first at a distance, then in all the everyday spots where you hang out. Finally you will be able to handle the responsibility of a ripening intimacy.

CHAPTER FIVE

GETTING TO KNOW EACH OTHER—IN PUBLIC, SLOWLY

THE "quick-draw" young men show up in every generation. These are the guys who brag about how fast they can move with a woman—any woman. Randy was one of them. He was a friend of mine, and he named the women in our high school with whom he could have sex any time, including some who were publicly steady girlfriends of top guns in the school.

Even then, I was baffled by Randy's recreational sex adventures. I had been dating the most beautiful woman in school. Randy and I were 15 and Leanna was a year ahead. He whispered to me before one of our classes opened. "I'll furnish the condoms if you want to have some fun with Leanna." At 15, I didn't have a great way of explaining, but I managed to say, "Hey thanks, but you don't know me at all. I'm not going to be having sex with her."

Randy's mother was in her third marriage. Her kids, with two sets of last names, rode the bus to our school. They were all beautiful people, but I know now that Randy's vision of a "lifelong exclusive relationship" had been warped by the insecurity of losing his father to an early divorce, and by being in a home where he was emotionally beat up almost daily. In a way, his popularity and his social ease were a miracle. But Randy left two pregnancies behind in his senior year, and in those pre-abortion days the young women did not finish school with us. I knew it then, but it makes more sense to me now: both of those beautiful girls were from father-absent and emotionally-damaging homes.

If you are a son of divorce or have survived in an alcohol-abusing household, or if you have been shaken by any other really terrible experience that has happened in your home, you may want to look at chapter 8. It is entitled, "Coming Back When Things Go Wrong." Then, come back, because I'm going to share the secrets I know about how to develop a "lifelong, exclusive bond" with that woman of your best visions!

THE MYSTERY OF BONDING

I'm not talking about what happens with model glue! In this sense, "bonding" refers to the powerful attachment that occurs between people when they have long-term or powerful experiences together. Parent-child attachment is easy to understand because of the time they invest in close contact. "Birth bonding"—that attachment that takes place between parents and their newborns—enhances the parent-child relationship for a lifetime. We now know that the first two-and-a-half hours of life are critical bonding minutes for both parents and the newborn baby. Both the parents and the baby will be more peaceable with each other. The baby cries less, and the parents worry about the child less if they have skin, eye and voice contact in spontaneous exchange during that critical first couple of hours.

Friends are often "bonded" by painful experiences. Victims of a hurricane or an earthquake, or hostages taken prisoner, often develop amazingly strong attachments that bring them together for the rest of their lives.

"Birth bonding"—that attachment that takes place between parents and their newborns—enhances the parent-child relationship for a lifetime.

But "pair bonding" is the best of bonding. This bonding looks very much like birth bonding. In fact, young adults are likely to make pair bonds that closely resemble the strength of the bonding they had with their parents as young children. A well-bonded adult from a healthy family, for example, breaks away from childhood dependency much like a bird leaving its nest. He becomes free and forms a marriage bond easily. These healthy teens or young adults rarely get involved in ugly power struggles with their parents.

FATHER ABSENCE AND BONDING

You can almost always predict what kind of a marriage partner anyone is going to make by listening to the way they talk with their parents. If a young woman is consistently in high-voltage emotional tension with her father, you can count on it: She will create a similar pattern with you. This is true of girls who have been abused as well as of those who could never quite find a way of winning their fathers' love in healthy ways. Some girls who have lost their fathers tend to be unsure of how to deal with a male and are shy and insecure. Others are desperately reaching out to fill that big void in their lives. They need fathering and will try to get it from you.

Shy young women are often mysteriously unavailable to anybody. The more outgoing, aggressive ones are the most difficult to spot. They seem like the answer to your prayers for a loving woman. Any healthy young man is eager to be touched and to respond by touching. But she may be "skin hungry" from a deformed childhood—and not driven by love for you. So this scenario is especially deceptive, since a young teenage guy tends to be starving himself for touch—he often pulls away from hugs and kisses from family and friends. In this appropriately starved state, he is likely to welcome the easily available woman with her need to be cuddled, kissed and touched. The really desperate "father absent" girls follow a deeper secret agenda. This is often the plot line of their reasoning:

- I lost the only man in my life.
- I will replace him.
- Any man will do.
- I am so desperate, I need my man now!
- To get him quickly, I will get pregnant by him.
- Even if he leaves me, at least I will have his baby.
- I will pray that my baby will be a boy.
- Then I will raise me a man.

I have worked with enough teens, young adults and older folks to have heard this story from 17-year-olds and from 50-year-olds. "You described exactly what was driving me," one good woman told me. "My father was a pastor and was always gone—meeting other people's needs. How I wanted him to pay attention to me. So I went after Richard, trying to replace my daddy. I was pregnant when we married, and it has taken us nearly 20 years for me to stop being the 'abandoned little girl' and to let Richard be my husband and lover instead of my 'father.'"

CRAZY BONDING

"Crazy bonding" happens in families or between couples when they mix any form of abuse, stress or selfish desires into the relationship. If any person is so needy as to manipulate—to control someone by jealousy or rage or to twist the relationship to meet his or her own needs—the bonding is flawed. If there is abuse—emotional, physical or sexual—the bond is often set up with super glue! I call it "crazy bonding" because even though the relationship is destructive, neither person seems able to get out of it.

Abused children, for example, often cannot leave home to go to college or live far away from their abusing parents as adults. They are always "coming home" to the abuse. They would rather accept the abuse they know rather than risking what's out there in this wild world. Abused children tend to be more dependent, and eventually are more likely to be carbon copies of the abuser: They will be abusers when it is their turn. So try not to dance the dance of "crazy bonding."

HEALTHY BONDING

I want to outline the best of all possible pair bonding scenarios for you. These "steps" or progressive phases of intimacy will unfold slowly and completely for you. But here's the bottom line: You do not need to study them in a book or to memorize the sequence. Simply be an honest and healthy man, take your time and watch the mystery of the pair bond unfold. I've adapted Desmond Morris's "12 steps" of pair bonding for you. I describe them in this chapter and the next, dividing the 12 steps into two major parts.

Your lifelong exclusive marriage will find you enjoying *all of the 12 steps* for the remainder of your life. They arrive singly, slowly and progressively. But once you have completed your work on a single step, it potentially belongs to the two of you forever—unless the entire structure collapses and you are devastated with the losses involved.

There are actually four levels of bonding, with three steps each. They include these unfolding opportunities:

Steps One Through Six
A. The entry gate to a potential lifelong relationship.
B. Building the foundations for exclusive commitment.

Steps Seven Through Twelve
C. The interior mansion your bonded marriage will inhabit and furnish for a lifetime.
D. The exclusive fortress and private chamber appears last and is absolutely protected, safe and exclusive.

Notice that the first six steps need to be built in public. They *require* public surveillance not only to keep you going slowly on the road to ultimate intimacy, but to remind you of the wonderful choice the two of you are making—when compared with the rest of the folks around. This public environment where you can see day after day that you have chosen the finest partner in the crowd is crucial for the lifelong bond.

Now let's take a look at those first two sets of three steps.

ENTRY GATE TO THE PAIR BOND

Keep in mind that these bonding steps are not something somebody "invented" to teach you how to make an exclusive, lifelong bond. Each are what careful observers have found are true everywhere, in every culture, when a man and a woman form that mysterious, lifelong, exclusive bond. So, if you have felt the first rush of attraction for a special person, you will recognize the powerful and good sequence of the "Entry Gate" as you look at the first three steps:

Step 1. *Eye-to-body.* "Wow! Where have you been all my life? Has she stepped out of heaven or what?" There's a sudden rush of surprise and excitement when you see that girl of your dreams. She may have grown up next door or have just arrived from a lost desert island in the Pacific. It makes little difference. She will look new and special. When Cupid strikes with the arrow of "eros," you flip head over heels for her. This unbelievably wonderful dream captures your full attention. She becomes singular. Nobody on earth compares with her at this moment. Unless you have been sexually abused, there will be no sexual content to this first sighting. There will be plenty of sexual imagination later, but not now. You sense that you do not yet *know* her, and that task of getting to know her is what pulls your eyes out of their sockets, trying to fill up your senses with this vision of possibilities for the rest of your life.

Step 2. *Eye-to-eye.* In the crowded place someone else is looking. She is enveloping you with her eyes. *What good timing,* you think! And helping to make it happen is the fact that through the mystery of the small brain voltage that passes through the eyes, you can almost always turn someone's eyes to you—simply by looking at them. "I feel like somebody is watching me" is often more than a feeling—it's a reality. So you turn instinctively to meet a pair of eyes! Later I'll walk you through the great love passages of the Bible, but sneak a preview now if you like, by looking at the ways the Old Testament book, Song of Songs reports this adoration of the eyes in chapter 1:15: "How beautiful you are, my darling! Oh, how beautiful! Your eyes are doves." Or look at 4:9: "You have stolen my heart, my sister, my bride; you have stolen my heart with one glance of your eyes."

Step 3. *Voice-to-voice.* When the eyes have met, all civilizations require a next step. However clumsily you do it, you *must* speak to her. You frantically seek out someone

Remember that building a healthy friendship is always enhanced if you can develop it in the middle of trusted friendships.

who knows both of you. "What is her name?" you long to know. If you are very lucky there is a gracious gift of an introduction—offered by the mutual friend. But you will find a way. In the best scenario, you approach her flanked by friends well-known to you, and you offer something like this: "My name is Jeff James, and these are my friends, Joe Johnson and Jack Jordan. I don't think I've seen you before." You have created space for her, and it includes space for a few friends to be introduced, too. Remember that building a healthy friendship is always enhanced if you can develop it in the middle of trusted friendships.

You can take it from there. Count on it: If she was gazing at you, she will be able to respond if you find your voice first. Both of you will feel healthier, more complete, as you take charge with quiet dignity. In the "worst case" scenario young boys are likely to pull a prank, drop a bag of pop-corn or create a scene in which the first speech is out of embarrassment or retaliation. Perhaps any speaking is bet-ter than none, but immature social moves rarely get a relationship off on the right foot. Go for it! Begin that search for the lifelong, exclusive relationship you long for, but do it the *right* way.

The "voice-to-voice" phase sets in motion the *communication* so critical in the healthy development of a bonded marriage. Men who have not established a reputation for being "verbal" suddenly find they can talk. I've known boys who had hardly composed one complete sentence in a year around their parents to suddenly burst into coherent speech with a girl. "Silent types" are no longer silent. You'll know that bonding is working when you suddenly find words to speak. What's more, you may be evoked to writing love notes, even poetry. Do it! Develop your communication and affectional skills while the motivation is bubbling up and overflowing. They will serve you very well for the remainder of a rich lifetime.

And use the telephone. Talking is more important than being under the stress of dating. Write notes, letters, friendship messages, poetry and songs. Give yourself permission to put your attention into language.

What next? OK—so it will likely be years before you get serious about picking your one-and-only. Still, even as you first begin to notice that the opposite sex seems to be getting more attractive than obnoxious, it will be a good idea to know what's been discovered about the mystery of bonding.

FOUNDATIONS FOR THE PAIR BOND

The next three steps involve simple and light touching. Desmond Morris and Melvin Konner, both of whom have studied pair bonding in many animal and bird species as well as among humans, are able to describe how important the bonding ritual is. Konner, for example, observes that among the "exclusively monogamous pair bonding species," the pair bonding ritual is very deliberate, with plenty of opportunity for either one to abandon the relationship. In exclusively monogamous bird species the courtship ritual includes building the nest—everything completed before breeding occurs.

I sometimes think maybe God created all species exclusively monogamous—one male with one female—but that evil damaged most of the species and their ability to bond exclusively. With human marriages breaking up in tragic numbers, we may decide it is worthwhile to pay attention to our inner vision and deep needs and to build the bond slowly, deliberately and with profound respect for the nonrenewable resources: ourselves. You must guard against following some clever scheme into becoming prematurely sexual. As the relationship matures, you will still find pleasure in visually sighting each other, in eye-to-eye contact and in endless voice-to-voice talking. Look at these foundation steps in the pair bonding sequence.

Step 4. *Hand-to-hand.* First touch between a man and a woman is almost always the touch of hands. In a crowd, the hands touch in order not to lose each other. Reaching out for each other is automatic: The hands link up. Even though the reaching out is for the practical reason of hanging on—to cross the street, to negotiate the traffic as you rush toward seating at the concert or to be sure of places together in the choir or the auditorium—the electric sensation that strikes you when hands touch is a bonding touch.

There is this magic with every new step in the bonding sequence, but first touch is sure to trigger its chemical high. The brain releases endorphins that instantly set off tingling sensations centered in your chest. These are often felt near the sternum in the middle of your chest. It's common for you to make a slight gasp as if you need more air. The brain chemicals are bonding the moment in permanent memory. If we could combine this kind of brain chemistry with academic studies, we could remember everything!

The hands will always be important in our relationship, so it is right that they are the first connection. By some estimates, one-third of all of your nerve endings are housed in your hands. Human hands are especially created for communication.

Step 5. *Arm-to-shoulder.* Desmond Morris found that all humans move next to connect in the first ownership gesture by which one of the pair will pull the other close by vice-gripping the arm around the partner's shoulder. Notice that both are still facing forward, as in "hand-to-hand," but the gesture tells everyone that this is a couple.

High and visible, the arm around the shoulder is a body link specifically serving notice on everyone present that these two people are joining in a special way. If they are of approximate equal height, the arms often entwine as both of the partners vice-lock the other's shoulders. As with the hands, this posture brings with it enormous brain chemical enjoyment. "I am loved. I am wanted. I have value!" is always an occasion for celebration.

Step 6. *Arm-to-waist.* Now the vice-lock releases, the hand limply falls to the waist. When both partners take this posture, the elbows cross behind their backs and the couple is "X-linked" together. It is common now for their heads to tuck down. They seem to be studying the ground a lot. They pull away from the crowd. They seem oblivious to other people. At Step Three, voice-to-voice, they were on the phone to each other, sometimes endlessly. Now they are talking, talking, talking while locked in the X-link.

While the Step 3 voice contact focused endlessly on gossip, "nothing things" their parents would have thought trivial, the conversation now is dead serious. It is serious because it is clearing the way for "till death do us part" kinds of plans and promises. The conversation has a perpetual "what if" tone, but the topics are "forever things." These are the Step 6 agendas somewhere in your future:

- How soon could we marry?
- Can we become adults and also please our parents and families?
- Waiting to be sexual until we are married.
- How many children?
- The kind of birth control to use in planning them.
- Beliefs, synchronizing religious commitments.
- Career plans.
- Education plans.
- Past relationships, killing off the ghosts.
- Personal or family scandals—share now or find out later?
- Review entire past life, knowing the whole story?
- Meeting and accepting the whole relatives chain.

Most marriages that end in divorce have failed because the couple did not take the time to work through these Step 6 agendas. But the super marriages I see inevitably involve couples who took the ultimate risks of knowing: They revealed their worst secrets, fully aware that this "knowing" could end the relationship.

I said recently to a couple just a month away from their marriage: "You have done your homework. The ruins of your painful past lives have been fully disclosed, and the bulldozer of understanding has leveled them. There are no surprises to explode your trust latter on. And the ghosts that might have inhabited those old and shame-filled memories have been exposed. You have listened and you have completely forgiven each other. The ruins are now compacted into a solid foundation for this final, lifelong relationship."

COMMIT OR BREAK UP NOW!

I cannot stress too much the importance of these "foundation" steps. The final one, Step 6, is what I have called "the last exit on the freeway of love." If either person breaks the relationship after Step 6, the result will have the same effects as divorce. Grief must work its way out of "denial," into anger, through bargaining, burrow through depression and finally come to acceptance and hope that there is life after the loss. So if another relationship is pursued to seal off the loss through actual denial of loss effects, we can be sure the future will be inhabited by the ghost of the lost relationship—the divorce effect.

Here is another image I sometimes use. Imagine that the pair bonding steps are markers along the runway as this jumbo jet plane is rumbling along for a take off. "Rotation" occurs at the end of the work you are doing in Step 6—at the end of this foundation phase of the relationship. This is the point of no return. The plane cannot be stopped and kept on the ground when Step 7 appears. Beyond this point the relationship will crash and burn if either has to leave. Both people, and perhaps others, will be injured and the scars can last a lifetime.

It is not surprising that the "Romeo and Juliet" syndrome has reached epidemic proportions in our time. What the news reports rarely mention is what the communities learn later: The teen suicide was related in someway to a relationship that went bad or to the inability to get the intimacy calendar and the real world calendar to match. Be sure to keep your friends talking if they are hurting by a broken bonding experience.

When pair bonding is kept before public witnesses during these first six steps, and when you have seen the striking quality of your chosen partner when compared to everyone else, you know the choice is both right and final.

The best bonded marriages are those that became "engaged" when the Step 6 work was largely done. At this point you are ready for the serious business of putting the final seal on the relationship. This will require substantial private time. The last half of the pair bonding steps lie beyond the view of many people. Indeed, you will find that your preferences have changed radically. Instead of wanting "time with the boys" regularly, you eagerly invest time with your future wife. Tell your guy friends to wait, you will return after two of three years into the marriage, and will continue at an adult level the excellent friendships you established with them during the preteen and junior high years. Males who are torn between their pack of friends and their fiance are men whose boyhood work is not yet done. Normally, the intensive peer friendships are invested between ages 10 and 15, and the healthy male takes his skills at friendship, at disclosure and honesty into his exclusive, lifelong marriage pursuit.

In chapter 6, we will look at the couple's private and personal agendas. These are the remaining six pair bonding steps and the tasks they require as you are going to be building that exclusive, lifelong marriage.

CHAPTER SIX

ACHIEVING THE ULTIMATE BOND

IN the last chapter I began describing Desmond Morris's "12 steps of pair bonding." I discovered them in his book *Intimate Behavior*. As a zoologist with special interest in how animals mate and raise their young, he includes humans in his "zoo." I don't think he knows that Creation comes from the hand of a God who loves intimacy. You can tell that it does, because it's easy to take Morris's 12 steps and put them together with Genesis 2 and the beautifully unfolding set of steps: leave parents; cleave or begin bonding to your partner; then find yourselves naked together without shame.

Desmond Morris has studied human intimacy and its development mostly because of his interest in how a species survives. He would tell you that if anything ever happens to weaken human pair bonding—the special lifelong, exclusive monogamous bond between a man and a woman—the species will be in danger of extinction. It takes about 15 years to launch a healthy kid who can bond and start over in a new exclusive family setting. And if life were simpler, 15-year-olds could marry easily. But from about 13 to 20, most of us need to grind out the complicated skills of dealing with a high-tech, high-priced culture before we marry. We've got to get our bonding right and be ready for marriage, because if bonding breaks down, it is your future kids who will suffer. If they suffer from abandonment or abuse, it is their potential bonding that is likely to be damaged too. Their future sexual behavior is more likely to be promiscuous or rapist or compulsive than if the kids came from an exclusive love relationship between father and mother. It is not inevitable, as you will see in chapter 8, "Coming Back When Things Go Wrong," but across the species or across any human culture, it is easy to see symptoms that pair bonding may be in trouble.

When you look around you, or in the mirror, you will be able to name young men and women who are facing this unusual risk. Stop and study this chapter, then stand in front of your own private mirror and have a conversation with yourself. You may even want to have a solidly imaginary conversation with the woman of your dreams whom you may not yet have even met. Promise her the kind of healthy man who can form an exclusive, lifelong bond. And use your influence among your friends. Ask them questions: "What do you really want for the rest of your life? Do you want exclusive lifelong loving or a series of divorces and the lonely life of the singles scene?"

FOR A LIFETIME?

You can have a bond that will last a lifetime but you've got to work at it *right now*. How? Develop a pattern in your search for intimacy that will forever change your behavior. Choose a winning courtship and marriage style that will ensure success. This "sure-fire formula" will help you achieve your goal for exclusive, lifelong intimacy, and will virtually guarantee that you will not abandon your wife and children. Check this out. You may think it is worth taking Desmond Morris's research seriously. Here are some of his observations:

1. *Make each step in the pair bonding sequence a place to stay awhile.* Move so slowly that you become completely relaxed with intimacy at Step 4, hand-to-hand, before moving to the ecstasy of Step 5, for example, arm-to-shoulder.

2. *Skip no steps.* Pay no attention to TV, movies or to the fast talk of your friends, who are running all of the pair

If anything ever happens to weaken human pair bonding—the special lifelong, exclusive monogamous bond between a man and a woman—the species will be in danger of extinction.

bonding red lights in order to get the sexual buzz of the later steps. If steps are skipped, like missing key training for an Olympic career, the bond will be profoundly damaged and is likely to break.

3. *Value the people involved.* You have been given this most amazing capacity to form an exclusive bond with *one person.* Fooling around just for kicks would be a little like trashing your own home, or torching the sports car of your dreams. The exception is this: A house or a car can be replaced. There will never be another *you* or another *her*, and your children will have no second chance for honest and healthy parents. The two of you are *nonrenewable resources*; so treat yourselves well.

4. *Avoid intimate, extended-time kissing* until Step 7. If the lips touch the other person before the work of Step 6 is finished, it is important to keep the kissing at the "conventional" level. That means, kiss her quickly in arrival

or departure rituals, much as you may kiss your parents, because of their importance to you as their son.

In chapter 5 I outlined the first six steps of pair bonding. You will need to develop them in the normal social traffic in which you move as a healthy individual. Keep your circle of friends close while you are locating the woman of your dreams and beginning to find out whether the two of you are "for keeps." Now, in this chapter, I want to walk you through the final six steps that will consummate the bond (the ultimate completion you've dreamed about) and seal it for a lifetime. Remember that the engagement, plans for a wedding date and synchronizing family connections were all negotiated as a part of Step 6. At Step 6, with all of its candor, shared secrets and serious planning, it was healthy to hear yourself saying, "Here we've been talking like we are getting married, and I haven't formally asked you to marry me. Will you?"

I cannot stress too much that this "Do the work, *then* ask the formal question" is an excellent sequence. It means that nobody is following a "cue sheet," but that both of you are following the good, healthy bonding procedures that are written deep in the core of your personalities.

The work of the final six steps is so intensely personal that you will now tend to pull away from the crowd and seek out the privacy you need to complete your exclusive, lifelong bonding process. As you sense your need for more private space, keep your hormones and your bonding sequence from running away by doing this:

• Make a promise to avoid absolute privacy.

• Make it a rule that parents and friends do not abandon you and devastate you by creating too much privacy. Announce to them that they are free to walk in any time. This strategy creates a "community" of family and friends whose casual presence can keep you from rushing these final, slow cementing/bonding steps.

• Plan your time together with intentional and active nonsexual events.

• Spend your endless conversation hours with witnesses around you. The shopping mall or the all-night restaurant are ideal. In a crowd you can get a completely confidential environment and still have "anonymous" supervision from the masses around you.

THE PAIR BOND'S INTERIOR MANSION

First touch hand-to-hand occurred at Step 3. The physical contact was light in the arm-to-shoulder and arm-to-waist steps, too. Now your couple posture changes. You have been side by side until now, but with Step 7, you turn facing each other:

Step 7. *Face-to-face.* Desmond Morris calls this step "mouth-to-mouth." He uses the title to stress the importance of waiting until the first six steps have been built before engaging in intimate, extended kissing. Morris points out that intimate kissing serves the purpose of "immunization." Benign bacteria from each person's digestive system are exchanged in extended open-mouth kissing. This protects you when you visit her "tribal headquarters" and eat the meals laced with her family's bacteria. The similar kissing of newborns is essential to start up their digestive systems with bacteria compatible to the home to which parents will take the baby.

Desmond Morris's caution is important to you because most teen and young adult bonds today are fatally flawed by premature intimate kissing. Extended kissing triggers sexual arousal. Once sexual arousal is experienced, the unfinished work of Steps 1 through 6 tends to be abandoned. If you don't go slowly in the first six steps, you'll end up getting too close too soon, and a prematurely physical or sexual relationship is almost certain to occur. It will tend to be shallow and deformed by an instrumental, "for kicks only" friendship. Such a relationship predicts a breakup that is messy and a heartbreak romance in every way. It simply has not built a lifelong bond.

But Step 7 in a healthy relationship sets up far more face-to-face intimate behavior than kissing. Now the cou-

> **Fooling around just for kicks would be a little like trashing your own home, or torching the sports car of your dreams. The exception is this: A house or a car can be replaced. You are a nonrenewable resource; so treat yourself well.**

ple—with total trust and with childhood and past secrets revealed—can give their eyes to each other. For the rest of your lives, keep this face-to-face inspection time a ritual on a daily basis. No deception, no inappropriate secrecy can survive if the eyes meet and all questions are answered. Couples married for 50 years or more typically hold each other at arm's length and study the face in order to draw strength from each other's faces, especially the eyes. If you want to be an honest person, give your wife regular opportunity to look deeply into your eyes. Sit across from her, not beside her, for meals. Turn toward her when she is talking, even if she is talking to the children or to someone else. Watch her with your private, vulnerable face—not your public, "game face."

By Step 7 in a relationship, the two know each other so well that they read more from the faces than from the words. Listen in as a nicely bonded, mature couple is talking privately. They rarely need to finish a sentence if they are facing each other. They can read infallibly the message written in the 18-square-inches of face that surround the eyes.

Scientists who study the brain-eye-speech connections now are suggesting that we can detect lying by watching specific eye movements in a speaker. Couples have known this for centuries. Parents knew it too, so they grabbed you as a little rascal, got to their knees and said to you, "Look at me and tell me again what you have been doing!"

But virtually all of the couple's face-to-face time is invested in positive nurturing of each other:

• Communication, extending the "knowing" boundaries.

• Receiving energy to build the dream you share.

• Accepting the assurance that the engagement is, indeed, secure.

Because the first six steps were so well built, Step 7 is a resting place, a secure place, in the sequence. There is less public "clinging" in the arm-to-waist style. The couple often stands free of each other, enjoys watching at a slight distance, even. They are sure of a wedding soon, of promises made to each other, of dreams celebrated and affirmed for each other. Now with all of these life issues settled, it is good to relax and simply be present to each other without clinging.

Step 8. *Hand-to-head*. In this facing posture, not only is intimate kissing and nonverbal reading of the eyes begun; eventually, the hands also go to the face and head. While talking, reading the eyes and face and bonding to the face, the hands involuntarily play games. With fingers they outline or highlight the facial and head features. Ears, mouth, nose and hair are easily targeted for gestures of caressing touch. These head and face games should be patented. They will be unique to you and your bride to be. No one will ever see these private, special games you have developed for each other. If, lying recovering on a hospital bed, you were to greet each other with these gestures, other guests would leave the room. We all recognize the private games of hand and face that a couple has developed, even though they were never exactly duplicated in our own repertoire of loving touch.

Hand-to-face touch is more sexually arousing than kissing, so the agenda is clearly visible now. If the "real world calendar" for your wedding day is far, far away, you will need to avoid the absolute privacy in which intimate gestures are appropriate. Don't go too far too soon. Set the rules to synchronize your "automatic intimacy needs calendar" with the wedding calendar, and keep your intimacy and responsibility integrity-bonded together.

Step 9. *Hand-to-body.* Knowledge of your partner's body increases day by day, and, without your knowing it, you will realize that you have a very complete knowledge of how she occupies space. Her shape, her weight distribution, the unique configuration of her fingers. Hands and feet—all of these are your domain. You could identify her by any of these parts alone. Desmond Morris stresses that this final step before naked and honest presentation does *not* include genital touch. But now the two of you are caregivers. If there is an injury or a pain, each will find the area and give it the healing touch or kiss. There is virtually no holding back because of feeling awkward or inappropriate. It is easy to see that the next step will be in the spirit of the oldest love story of all. Let me use honest and parallel terms for the woman and the man in my own translation of Genesis 2:25: "And the man and the woman were both naked and they were unashamed."

THE FORTRESS CHAMBER: ULTIMATE SAFETY

Hundreds of times I have heard it: "It was terrible. Everybody said they were doing it, so I found this girl and we had sex. But it was terrible!" Don't be fooled by others. There is simply no way for a man and a woman to have super intimacy without investing time in building the whole castle of love. You will see that these final three pair bonding steps can be absolutely awesome. But they must be reserved for full trust, legal security, public covenant and blessing, and patient exploration. Only then will you be sure to find yourselves easily "naked and without shame," in the positive, beautiful imagery of the Judeo-Christian doctrine of Creation.

It is worth sacrificing almost everything else to "get yourselves to the church on time!" However much you struggle with synchronizing the "real world calendar" and your "intimacy needs calendar," genital contact deserves to be enjoyed in a publicly celebrated marriage. Only those conditions provide solid emotional security for each of you and guaranteed proof that you are taking full responsibility for each other, now and forever. Unless you build the castle's fortress as a safe place visible to all but securely private for the two of you alone, insecurity will stalk your lives.

You will hear some talk about "sexual sin." You may hear about "fornication" and "adultery," for example. You can jump ahead to chapter 9 if you want to get to the root of the issue of sexual sin as the Bible describes it. But it is not as simple as naming sins. Sin is only a theological word meaning "DISASTER." Anything that is destructive is sin. So chapter 9 is entirely given to walking you through the Bible images and texts that celebrate the marriage and sexual relationship at the highest, most complete enjoyment.

You will find, if you open your own Bible and follow me through that chapter, that the Bible teachings are positive and true because they accurately describe the way things are! I had a theology teacher in college who used to shock me everytime he reminded me of that. He said, "Nothing is true *because it is in the Bible*. It is in the Bible *because it is true!*" So don't believe your friends' far-fetched stories of their sexual adventures. They are not going to escape the tragic consequences of their choices and their behavior simply because they don't know the word "sin." In the New Testament, the word translated "sin" actually means "missing the mark"—just as when an arrow misses a target. Just because we don't think about such "Bible talk" doesn't mean we won't get hurt when we "miss the target" God has for us. Actually, pagans may hurt worse, because they not only don't know how they hit DISASTER, but also do not have any idea how to be healed.

Now look at those final pair bonding steps that symbolize the best of intimacy:

Step 10. *Mouth-to-breast.* Here is where Desmond Morris gives up. As a zoologist he is baffled. No other species, not even one among the primates, behaves like the human male. A male, who began life suckling at his mother's breast, returns now to his wife's breast. It is a gesture of tenderness and trusting dependency, as if to say, *I need you. I draw strength from you. If you love me and believe in me I can be strong.* So when a man reduces himself to this gesture of absolute weakness and dependency, he is preparing himself for the tenderest experience of his life: sexual union with his exclusive woman.

Step 11. *Hand-to-genital.* Speech continues to fade as intimacy increases. The speaking portion of the brain tends to surrender now to the deep and almost instinctual rituals, which will consummate (bring to completion) the couple's sexual union. To "know" the person ultimately requires the exploration of the source of life and of ultimate pleasure. So the husband and wife admit each other to the most private secret—to know the miraculous genitals with their power for creating life and of giving the highest ecstasy lifelong.

Anyone who seduces a person to gain sexual contact without carefully and slowly building the steps of bonding will be sure to violate the other person, since the automatic rituals that move toward intercourse will take over and sex will happen. The result will be date rape, marriage rape or a bad scene that devalues your partner, endangers the emotional health of your sexuality as well as your mate's (not to mention that of your future spouses and children). The bottom line: Getting too close too soon leaves you loaded with guilt and shame.

Step 12. *Genital-to-genital.* Knowing your wife completely and her knowing you symbolizes the giving up of all privacy and secrets. The "two are becoming one" in every way. You now know each other through the careful building of the steps of intimacy. Penetration and the union of your bodies in sexual intercourse will be the best statement of your affection you have yet made. This ritual of loving will be your special symphony of commitment on your wedding day and for literally thousands of days throughout your marriage.

RISK-PROOFING YOUR MARRIAGE

Your instinctual sense of responsibility has told you to protect your woman, to be an honest man and to establish a home in which the two of you always will be safe. You will follow that best appetite. But if you want long-term risk-proofing for your marriage, here are bonding tips:

1. *Play all 12 strings on this instrument of lifelong loving.* Busy couples easily get bogged down with jobs, meals, children, even recreation and moonlighting. But protecting your marital bond requires time for face-to-face, voice-to-voice and hand-to-head exchanges and rituals. You can spot serious defects when the two of you no longer look into each other's face when speaking. The cure requires "starting over" and playing those early steps as the lower and foundational strings of your instrument of love.

2. *If your lives get busy, schedule time for each other as a top priority each week.* A healthy marriage can sustain some spaces in the togetherness, and since a few days apart make you more eager than before to be together you can literally "make up for lost days." Simply book extra time together, a getaway weekend or a special date. Focus in on each other, on listening with your eyes as well as your ears and on stroking face, hair and the body in nonsexual ways. Bonding is mostly communication, the knitting together of mind, affections, beliefs and values. Bonding takes time. There is no short cut.

In chapters 5 and 6 I have spread out the story of how two become one—the mystery of pair bonding. It is a beautiful story. And the internal mansion you will build together is more complicated than the visible bonding steps I've described. But only the two of you will be able to describe the texture and the quality of life inside the bond itself. You deserve to tell that story to each other. Your children and grandchildren will thank you for building well.

CHAPTER SEVEN

TIGER IN YOUR TANK!

My father posed a question for me early one morning. "Did I ever tell you about the day you were conceived?" he asked. We were milking cows before daylight. I was exactly your age, Jason, when he asked that question! I was glad I was hiding behind the flank of the cow when he asked it. He couldn't read the shock on my face.

I cleared my throat trying to hide my nervousness, and managed to respond calmly: "I don't think you ever did."

So he told me. My dad had to know that I had entered into my visible manhood. I was now slightly taller than he was. After all, I had grown nine inches in height during the last school year. Now this question! Of course he wasn't dumb. Dad talked to me about everything. He taught me everything he knew. Now, obviously, he was going to teach me something about my sexuality.

In my wildest imagination, I never thought a sex talk would begin like this! He was starting with my own conception—the heart of the sex issue: fertility. A "birds and bees" talk would have been less threatening—even laughable, considering what I had already discovered. At this point, I had literally lived on the farm around birds, bees, cattle, horses, pigs, sheep and abundant nearby wildlife. I knew about animal reproduction. Dad was right. It was *human* sexuality on which I was only vaguely smart and urgently curious.

FERTILITY

Dad taught me what he knew. And he made it personal. I am still impressed with his teaching ability. "I thought your mother might never sing again," he began. She had lost their first pregnancy. Then, two months later, under circumstances he described for me, I was conceived, and Mother was happy again. I was a "wanted child"!

I never told him about another lesson he taught me. That baby who was lost gave up its space to me. There would have been "no room in the womb" for my conception. I could never have been conceived if that first baby had gone to full term. Their second child wouldn't have been me; genetically, at least, those sperm and ovum would have been gone, wasted.

Wow! I almost didn't make it on to this planet.

Wow again! I need to live my life thankfully and fully—out of respect to a baby who didn't make it.

Dad taught me more than I thought possible about sex, fertility and life.

Dad didn't know then what I have only recently discovered: For every 100 girls who are conceived, about 160 boys are conceived. But making a baby boy is so very complicated that 54 of the boys will spontaneously "miscarry," and the baby is lost. This sometimes happens because the first cells to form get messed up and the baby can't make it and be well. I'll unravel this "boy making" task a little later.

Dad accidentally, or on purpose, set me up to respect fertility, to value conception, pregnancy and birth as major wonders of the universe. He never suggested that sex was dangerous, or that fertility could "get me into trouble." His approach to sex education was a gift that could set me up for life—in every way. I was impressed. He made it personal, serious and full of unfolding mystery—packaged exclusively for me!

Dad didn't have the technical vocabulary that you and I have, Jason, when he talked to me about everything sexual. If he had known more, I'm sure he would have found a way to teach me, just as he did, without embarrassing me or violating my privacy. As a teenager, I had some questions about a couple of things. The manhood adventure might have been richer and a bit easier if Dad had known how to describe them. I'm going to try to do that here. You can do an even better job for your sons and grandsons.

"WHAT ARE LITTLE BOYS MADE OF?"

There is a wonderful story that unfolds during the nine months when a baby is being created. The old nursery poem was wrong. Little boys are not actually made of "sticks and snails and puppy dog tails"! They are, instead, made of what I call "the Original Adam." As Genesis 2 reveals, everything that is in a male as well as in a female was packed in to one person. Then, at the ninth week, God "splits the Adam" to make a female or a male. And again as in Genesis 2, we all seem to be driven for our whole lives knowing that "it is not good" that Adam should be alone; so the hunger for "the other" sends us in search of love and a lifelong pair bond.

All babies develop the same for the first 10 weeks, so far as you can see. If you lost a baby anytime before the 12th week, it would appear to be a baby girl by all indicators. Boys and girls look identical as they are developing.

At five weeks you can see an open vagina and a pleasure "bump" at the top—obviously the beginning of the female system with its clitoris. But what we cannot see is that inside the baby there are a pair of ovaries in vertical position, side by side like tiny footballs. They are within the embrace of a "wishbone" made of the two fallopian tubes—called Müllerian ducts at this time. Anyone looking at this internal sex system would identify female parts.

SEXUAL PLEASURE

God must have known how tough it is to be human, especially when the going gets rough, when there are obligations, work and trouble everywhere. Next to the recharging energy you get from a full night of sleep, your capacity for sexual pleasure is the best renewal gift Creation built into you. And each person is so "magnetically" made that the best pleasure comes only through the presenting of sexual gifts I described in chapter 6. I called that pleasure union "The Fortress Chamber: Ultimate Safety," and the chapter title is "Achieving the Ultimate Bond."

It is fairly common for young boys and girls to discover their "pleasure centers" located in the genitals. Childhood masturbation—pleasuring through stimulating the genitals—most often happens accidentally. A child of only a few months or a few years is surprised and pleased to have discovered the pleasure.

The differences between the pleasure system in males compared to the pleasure system in females is rooted in the 9th to 12th weeks of fetal development as I explained. Boys and girls start out identical in sexual formation. Some marks of that beginning remain in adults. Since the fetus at nine weeks appears to be female, it is not surprising that every boy child carries breasts. Until pubescence, the upper torso of boys and girls look alike. The boy's body is formed from the "female format," as is obvious by that comparison.

Boy babies carry a bright red scar running the full length from the rectum, around the scrotum with its former ovaries now in place as testes or testicles. The scar continues up the underside of the penis. It was sealed by what I call the "glue of God" as the vaginal lips were closed to form the amazing "thermostat" sac to keep the sperm factory just the right temperature in cold weather and hot, and to wrap the penis in highly expandable material—just like the elastic vaginal lips in a baby girl, which will some day enlarge, we hope, to allow her to give birth to a baby.

The pleasure centers in girls and boys are "differentiated" profoundly. By the 15th week of fetal development the clitoris retreats and is enclosed inside the vaginal lips in the baby girl. But in a boy this "bump" enlarges and rises on the clitoral shaft, which forms the penis and encloses the urinary tract in the baby boy. So a young girl who discovers the pleasure center in her clitoris may not have a clear sense that she is touching genitals, since the pleasure is not connected to anything visible, or to any other body function. Boys, however, know where the pleasure comes from because, since first toilet training, they have been given a name for the penis. The pleasure center at the end of the penile shaft, remember, is the transformed clitoris in the early fetus. But the boy's urination regularly requires handling the penis, so the sensitive pleasure center gets accidentally stimulated very often.

So for boys there is no mystery about where the pleasure comes from. Besides, those powerful sensations are clearly associated with the privacy of the bathroom, as our parents teach us. Young girls are more likely to pleasure themselves anywhere they happen to be, and seem not to associate it with a need for privacy. Boys, very early, may tend to be more secretive about sexual things.

By the time their manhood arrives—full height, a daily beard, voice change and full-sized genitals—the young man is very aware of pleasure. The soft penis seems to have suddenly grown. It is enlarged by the massive doses of testosterone his testicles are producing. And at full arousal the length of the penile shaft matches exactly the distance from the base of the hand to the tip of the middle finger fully extended. This mysterious and magnificent proportion—much like the similar fact that your height matches exactly the measurement of the span from center fingertip to fingertip—can put you in awe of God's "fearfully and wonderfully made" creation. It also may make you cringe when violent boys or men invent finger gestures to suggest their crude sexual intentions.

When these body changes occur, most young men are both very secretive and private, but also are very pleased with the newly developing body. The young man's whole body is super masculine, a product of his skyrocketing androgen level. The male hormone peak runs typically from about age 16 to about age 30. His musculature "builds" best during this time because of these high hormonal charges, as well. While he will produce testosterone literally all over his epidermis (the outer layer of skin), especially the hair follicle areas, his testes are his main testosterone hormone factory—producing an average of 300,000,000 sperm each day. This incredible fertility gift loads tiny pouches called "seminal vasicles." As they become fully loaded, the erection-arousal process triggers easily.

It is common for a man during these peak years to be aware of sexual arousal several times each day. And during sleep there are full erections about every 90 minutes. These are connected to deep sleep and REM (rapid eye movement) signals of dreaming. Yet the dream content is rarely sexual as the erections occur.

Those baby boy ovaries that appeared by the fifth week will have now been coated with the mother's androgen chemicals. Then they were suctioned, pulled inside the Müllerian ducts and "swallowed" as they traveled down to the outside of the body. There they are clearly testicles and are housed in the lower section of vaginal lip material. This soft, elastic material becomes the scrotum or sac. It will act as the original "thermostat," guaranteeing to keep the testicles exactly three degrees cooler than normal body temperature—essential for producing mature and fast-swimming sperm. And the scrotum is marked by the continuing scar. You have seen it on every baby boy whose diaper you may have changed. It is a bright red scar—straight as a surgeon's incision—that is visible as it seems to divide the child's scrotum in half, down the center line of his body. The little boy has been "modified" out of the female model and he has scars to prove the journey he has been making.

RESPONSIBLE FOR PLEASURE

So welcome to manhood, Jason. You are entering an adult world full of potential for responsibility and pleasure that are magnificently "built in" to your fertility. I am wanting to salute you in the early days of your young manhood. I'm pleased to guide you into the wonderful world of being male, responsible and mature. And since you will quickly move to full male sperm production, you will be responsible for dealing with your fertility and doing that alone.

Your sister likely got parental help when she hit her first "period." And everybody treated this transition as normal, even showing her new respect for this mark of her arriving womanhood. Your dad would not, in his wildest crazy moment, ever tell her to "Stop ovulating and doing this messy menstruating until you are married!" Yet in worst cases a young man may be humiliated and shamed as crudely by parents—most often by a mother who hasn't understood and maybe even is repulsed by the male sex system, which is not at all like her own. If parents do not treasure their own differences and magnetically find the "other" attractive, they tend to send bad signals to their kids.

And in "best cases" most boys' arrival at manhood—signalled by first ejaculation of sperm material and followed up by occasional or frequent evacuations—is simply ignored in silence. Most young men eventually decide that "God didn't make a mistake" and that they were not created wrongly. But the silence you could interpret as disapproval of you or as family embarrassment or shame can often leave its deep wounds in the years from about 12 to 20.

This "tiger in the tank" of your new manhood deserves your special respect. Your sexual gift is your connection to one exclusive lifelong partner—the "dream" I celebrated with you in chapter 5. So the years between the arrival of your full adult sexual "charge" and your wedding day are entirely your responsibility. Here are some "pain alternatives" and probable consequences as you accept responsibility for your sexual energy and pleasure.

If you make sexual connections with other people before your lifelong partner—if you have premarital sex of any kind—your "bonding" will be vulnerable to three kinds of risks. Each predicts virtual lifelong pain.

• If your sexual bonding occurs without taking full responsibility for one another through legal marriage, you will be developing a pleasure appetite that is disconnected from the real world of work and responsibility. You will be at risk for an affair that is free of day by day responsibility—sex for kicks, not for intimate sharing.

• If your sexual bonding occurs early and powerfully but you cannot consummate marriage to cement the promises you made in your hearts, you are in for the "adultery effect." Adulterating your bonding means that you are at risk to carry the early "ghost" of that serious commitment like a "divorce" into your future marriage. A sexual relationship needs daily responsible care or it inevitably breaks, so the divorce effect is very predictable.

• Coming off of either of the first two examples, above, you would be at risk to have a series of sexual partners. If you become quickly sexual with several partners, you are

When the Christian doctrine of creation says, "The two shall become one flesh," it is easy to see that, sexually, the male is made to complete the female, and the female anatomy is the exact missing "mirror image" of the male.

at risk of slipping into the promiscuity pattern in which you and other people are only sexual bodies looking for union. This may be the most painful of all effects, because promiscuous people eventually become very lonely. They cannot maintain any relationship across time. Their bonding glue is neutralized and doesn't work after ripping loose from so many people.

In the opposite set of cases, if you abstain from sexual contact until marriage, you are also set for pain.

First, if you set your mind to ignore your need for intimacy and to steel yourself against an honest and very deliberate pursuit of a lifelong partner, you are at risk of over-protecting and paying the price of being cold and indifferent to people. The "Pharisee syndrome" makes harsh judgments against sinners who have sex, and from this high throne becomes cynical and hardened in pride. What is ironic is this: With his male hydraulic system, he is going to "go off" with a fertility explosion from time to time, and he is also vulnerable to cyclical struggles with masturbation at best, or pornography, prostitution or homosexual relief at worst.

Second, in the best of all probable worlds, the young man may make a peaceable covenant between himself and that unknown woman in his future, to go for sexual intimacy only in marriage. But the waiting, the cycles of hormonal elevation and the evacuation of the seminal system all leave the fellow with feelings of anguish and loneliness. "Will I live to see my wedding day?" becomes the primal wail of the healthy, covenant-bound young man. Religious young men often cry out asking God to delay the Second Coming of Jesus until they can marry and be sexual. Your system is a frequent reminder that you were made for intimacy and this solitary confinement feels like a prison in which you rot your young vitality away.

If you feel all alone in your struggle, read in 2 Corinthians 12:7-10 about the Apostle Paul's struggle with a "thorn in the flesh." "Three times," he writes, "I pleaded with the Lord to take it away from me. But he said to me, 'My grace is sufficient for you, for my power is made perfect in weakness.'" Don't be surprised if you feel the same, identical feelings of desperation and loneliness. The private notes and journals of the greatest religious figures reveal struggles with the sexual frustration of their lives.

So there is pain for you either way. But that is God's wonderful way of making you into a moral giant in a few years. So celebrate the good gift of Creation, and cry yourself to sleep alone sometimes. It is a good thing to ask God "Why?!" as you pay the price of waiting. Listen a lot to the pain of your peers who are dealing with the consequences of casual and easy sexual contact. And pray

God's grace of "ripening wisdom" on those who suffer alone and largely in silence, as you do.

So you got your sex system as a modification out of a visibly female body—as a "mirror image" of the female in every way. When the Christian doctrine of creation says, "The two shall become one flesh," it is easy to see that, sexually, the male is made to complete the female, and the female anatomy is the exact missing "mirror image" of the male. But the differences are so enormous that men will need to patiently study women, and women will need patiently to study men. It will be destructive for either to judge or to try to control the other on the assumption that "both are the same."

THE MALE MIND

Several interesting things happened to your fetal brain—as the boy was being created in your mother's womb. Between the 16th and 26th weeks of your development, your mother's androgens (male hormones) combined with testosterone from your own developing testicles to form a frost-like, chemical coating on the entire left hemisphere of your brain. The coating is God's way of masculinizing the brain so you can "think like a man." Men are able to "focus in" and give intense attention to anything, almost without distraction. But the "masculinizing" required killing off about 25 million fiber-optics-like connections between the left and the right hemispheres of your brain.

As you may know, it's this left hemisphere that is the speech center and generally dominant for right-handed people. So picture this: You have lost millions of fiber-optics connections between your left-brain speech and your right-brain feelings-emotions-beliefs-images-music needs. You may find it harder than girls and women do to put your right-brain judgments and decisions into words.

And when you remember that the left brain got the hormone coating, you will understand that boys' speech often arrives more slowly and with more problems. Nine out of 10 children in first grade speech therapy are boys. But you can treat this normal male development factor as a challenge, not a handicap. Remember, you can be "single

Between 10 and 14 it is important for boys to develop close male friendships. They share secrets and learn to trust their peers. This is an important rehearsal for searching for a confidential, close friendship with a life-mate.

minded"! But take this good news as a invitation to cultivate your "right mind," too, because everything that keeps you human, warm and kind gets processed there. For example, fill your head with music that makes you a gentle and gracious man.

On the other hand, another process in brain development usually gives boys better control over their bodies—better coordination. The "eye-hand" skill you use with your Nintendo or the arcade video games demonstrates that that "single minded" male brain can excel at eye-hand coordination.

Since the dosage of androgens varies greatly during brain development, males are more susceptible than females to being attracted to the opposite sex at widely varying ages. You may have passed through an "I hate girls" stage, as many boys do. Between 10 and 14 it is important for boys to develop close male friendships. They share secrets and learn to trust peers. This is an important rehearsal for searching for a confidential, close friendship with a life-mate. So the later teen years usually find the young man beginning that search.

It is quite common, too, for young men to feel confused, even worried, about their sexuality in their early and mid-teens. But if you can say yes! to the wonderful thing God has done in creating you a healthy male, you can put your best friends at ease too—both the young men and the young women. And you can help keep your friends moving with respect, even reverence, for the joy of growing up celebrating God's good gifts. Boys who get confused and worried about themselves tend to get harsh and rough and macho, and they are dangerous around girls. And some boys retreat, turning inward, and are very insecure. They can be victims of almost anyone who hunts them down for any purpose at all. So keep your eye out for these macho or those retreating guys around you. They need some of the good news you have.

Another wonder of brain development is that both boys and girls have been blessed by what is called "the myelinization of the central nervous system." The "myelin sheath" acts as insulation around the nerves, and actually speeds up messages between the brain and the rest of the body. As you reach pubescence, sexual maturity and sexual responsibility are somehow timed to arrive just as the final touches are being placed on this high speed thinking-and-acting gift. You will know that your "myelin sheath" is completed, right up to the correlation fibers of your central cortex, when the following signs appear.

1. You find yourself wondering where you came from, where you are going and what your life is for.

2. You sometimes ask yourself these and other questions as you stand in front of the mirror in the privacy of your bathroom, or when you are all alone anywhere.

3. You are reflective whenever you get quiet. Sometimes you make it a point to be around people because you don't like the negative thoughts you have about yourself if you are alone.

4. You wonder whether anybody out there respects you, whether anyone would love you for a lifetime, whether God exists and, if so, whether God understands, values and respects you.

These are wonderful and terrible agendas. They mean that you no longer are a little child. Welcome to the world of adult reality, adult responsibilities, adult priorities and to the maturity you have been yearning for.

STAND TALL!

Your new maturity looks great on you. I couldn't be happier with who you are or with the way you are wearing the mantle of your maleness. You have handled every "developmental task" with honor and distinction. You are competent to deal well with this central task of being yourself in a world gone crazy. Go for it!

CHAPTER EIGHT

COMING BACK WHEN THINGS GO WRONG

DAN is a young father for whom very few things went right. His father was both an alcoholic and a family abuser. When his mother divorced Dan's natural father and remarried, Dan felt lost in a new blended family. Much of the time it seemed to him like he got blamed when one of the step kids deserved the discipline or the scolding.

DEALING WITH ABUSE AND LOSS

Boys like Dan find a way to survive; Dan's way of surviving was to excel in school. He needed approval somewhere, and his teachers seemed to be safe adults. Their approval counted for a lot with Dan. But he felt ashamed of his background, his blended family that wasn't working out well.

Dan kept mostly to himself. The friendships healthy boys build during the years from about 10 to 13 simply didn't develop for Dan. He felt like a big zero—so inferior that he thought nobody would want to associate with him. But he had a deep hunger for a close friendship. That need simply didn't get met. I met Dan in his final year of graduate school, where he was preparing to be a minister. He was 24 years old, wondering whether there would ever be another human being on earth who would respect and value him.

WHEN CHILDHOOD IS FILLED WITH PAIN

In this chapter I want to outline three "case" stories, and for each I will describe "what went wrong" and then offer a way "to fix it."

The first case is that of Dan, with his painful family losses.

The second case will be that of Ron, whose hurt and pain clouded up his own sexual vision.

A final case will be that of Bob, whose anxious and competing parents locked him into "the child as pawn" position.

HEALING FROM ABUSE AND ABANDONMENT

Dan's family losses, including his natural father's alcoholism and his lack of bonding into a new family (called a blended family), are tragic and painful boyhood experiences. Look at what went wrong for Dan by checking out what his unmet needs were. These were his losses:

1. His natural father, who could have been the hero of Dan's life, was abusive and alcoholic. Dan lost the affection, the model, the praise and the companionship of his dad. Dan was robbed of what every boy deserves. This loss put a deep hole in Dan's memory. It is a "black hole" that Dan feels as "inferiority," because the abuse and then the abandonment tell him something like this: *You are not worth loving! If you were a better kid, your dad would control his alcoholism and stop hitting on you and your mother.* Boys whose fathers abuse or abandon the marriage and the family often struggle to get this "hole"

plugged and start to respect themselves. And what is worse, perhaps, is the fear the boy often develops. *If men are jerks,* a boy often thinks, *I am a boy, I'll probably grow up to be a jerk, too!* Childhood and adolescent depression among boys is often rooted in this fear that *I'll be just as worthless and abusing as Dad.*

2. Dan lost the full attention and concern of his mother when she remarried. This was a big disappointment to him. And now he had to try to please a man who was replacing his real dad, and who seemed to love his own set of children more than he loved Dan. The message Dan could construct in this new family was something like this: *Mother married this man; I didn't. Maybe he didn't really want me, but I just came in the package deal. His children seem really special to him, but I seem to get all the raw deals and dirty work. Besides, when I was the only kid, it was like I was a partner to Mom. Now that there are two older kids and a younger one, I'm just in the middle of the pack, and I feel lost.*

Can you feel what Dan must have been feeling? In the first marriage, he felt abused and abandoned, and that drove him into a black hole of inferiority and feelings of shame—wanting to hide the truth about himself from everybody. In the second home, Dan felt unwanted, unrespected and exploited. These are further blows to Dan's sense of self-value or self-respect.

COUNTING THE LOSSES

Let me give some basic rules as foundations for the healing strategies I am going to offer you. Here are some definitions and rules about self-respect or self-esteem:

1. "Self-concept," "self-respect" and "self-esteem" are tricky terms, because everyone's sense of self-worth comes from other people—not from themselves. How a

baby is handled, talked to and protected from bad things that happen to people builds "self-value" into the child. Children who begin life in a family where abuse is present get "no value" messages about themselves. Homes filled with emotional abuse—where name-calling, ridicule and obscenities are hurled at each other—are bankrupting each other's self-respect. When an abuser or a screamer

Self-worth or self-respect—the "sense of self"—gets its major shape during the early years of life.

uses such words, it is a sure sign they are calling you exactly what they think *they* are—a big zero.

2. Self-worth or self-respect—the "sense of self"—gets its major shape during the early years of life. Adults who have been secure, respected and treasured by their parents in infancy and early childhood can take abuse as adults without being devastated. "When Charlie swore at me, I thought, *He is really hurting!*" This is the response of a man who has a healthy sense of self-respect.

3. People with "low self-respect" will tend to show low respect for other people. They will meet sarcasm with sarcasm, obscenity with obscenity. So if there is one devastated person in a family, it is easy for everybody else to "dance the dance" of mutual devastation until everybody is caught spiraling downward into a black hole of worthlessness. You can hear the value of persons coming through in every family as they talk with each other. Learn to listen and to see how each family member is responding.

4. People who experience family devastation tend to make one of two responses. One group, the honest and reflective ones, tend to suffer from extreme inferiority.

They withdraw, as Dan did, and feel worthless and do not attempt to make friends. They drift deeper into isolation. People like Dan are likely to be victims of depression, or they will suffer from feelings of shame and be apologetic whenever someone tries to affirm them or be their friend. "Inferiority" is the unspoken middle name of these reflective, devastated men.

The other group turns "macho." To compensate, these guys use a false mask and skillfully deceive us into thinking they are strong, cool and truly masculine. They tend to put on a happy or a strong face and meet the world behind this mask. Every macho male who swaggers, threats, acts cocky and throws his weight around to get what he wants is a damaged, low self-respect male. His obscenities, his large intake of alcohol, drugs and sex are attempts to compensate, masking his own emptiness.

The macho male may try to use his arsenal of abusive weapons to devastate any healthy male or any honest "inferiority" male. These weapons may consist of name-calling, sarcasm or the use of obscenities. One macho strategy is to do violence, even to rape. One theory behind the assassination of prominent figures is that an insecure macho male felt he had to bring down a man who was calm and confident, and a public hero.

FILLING THE CUP OF SELF-ESTEEM

Macho boys who become men keep bumping people away through their harshness. They dump friends before they get dumped. If they do not face their emptiness and need for healing, they grow increasingly isolated from everybody. Such men simply will not take the risks necessary to establishing long term friendships, or be vulnerable enough to risk being hurt in love and marriage. But if they can ever face the truth of their acting tough as a strategy for survival and self-protection, they can be healed of their devastation in the same way the "inferiority boy" can be healed after he has turned into a man.

Since self-respect is actually the "cup" into which we have received respect from others, healing demands trusting some other people. Most of us arrive at our teen years and our adult careers with some scars on our self-respect. We have had a close brush with abuse or abandonment of some kind. So what I am offering here is a strategy that all of us need for the rest of our lives, in one degree or another. Here are some steps to take to fill "the cup of self-respect."

1. Give yourself permission to look for a "mentor." A mentor could be any person you admire and with whom you openly make arrangements to learn what he or she knows. At about 12 or 13 most boys automatically find themselves admiring a teacher, coach, pastor or neighborhood adult who is their "model." This is true even for boys whose fathers have been their childhood models. But for boys with a devastated family experience, the mentor can be a lifesaver and a true "surrogate" or substitute dad or mom.

2. Take an hour in the privacy of your room and list the losses you feel. "I felt abused, abandoned or devastated when I ..." will get you started. "I felt inadequate, inferior or ashamed when..." takes you further. "What I need more than anything else..." may wrap up your best hopes. Try giving yourself permission to tell the truth on paper. Then lock it up or carry it in your wallet as your own personal life agenda. You are now ready to take the next step.

3. Ask yourself whether your mentor could handle your secrets. Your mentor needs to be strong enough that you can imagine telling the whole thing and the person would tell you, "You're the most courageous guy I have ever met." Watch carefully. Read faces, especially eyes, and lis-

ten to how the person talks about people who suffer publicly from the feelings you have hidden away inside. Jesus once cautioned: "Don't cast your pearls before swine." He was warning that a dangerous person, like a hungry dumb pig, is likely to "trample your pearl" of suffering, then turn on you and "rip you to shreds." Since you have already suffered enough, you don't need to be ripped to shreds again.

Every healthy person needs a "network" of honest friendships that are based on absolute respect for each other.

4. Intentionally look for a casual moment to drop the first piece of truth. Give your chosen person a small piece of your pain first, before you risk everything. Can you hear yourself saying to this mentor you have chosen—a teacher, a pastor or some really mature peer—"I've decided to deal with some of my childhood pain before it messes up my whole life"?

5. Once you have opened the door to reveal your secret pain, reach out to a few other people and do the same with them. Every healthy person needs a "network" of honest friendships that are based on absolute respect for each other. When you have the network you need for a lifetime, it will tend to look like this:

a. It will include about five people from your immediate family. If you cannot locate five pairs of honest eyes, five people with absolute respect for you among parents, brothers and sisters, you can pick up a few others from the other groups. But promise yourself that you will be a husband who creates an open home where your wife and children are honest and have unconditional respect for people. You can then repair this side of your network.

b. There will also be about five people from your extended family. These are cousins, aunts, uncles and grandparents. Imagine yourself saying to these select relatives the same thing you wanted to say to your admired mentor: "I've been through a lot, but I've decided to face it and get on with being healthy in spite of it." If you cannot identify about five people in this part of your network, look for a way to enlarge one of the remaining groups.

c. You need about five people from your "work place" acquaintances. This may be school, your job or wherever you invest your work-week time. Again, think of the faces you can trust, the honest people who will encourage you in your journey to healthy adulthood.

d. Finally, you will need about five people from your lifelong collection of neighbors, childhood friends and classmates. You need to check them out in the same way, slowly revealing your decision to put your pain to rest.

What may surprise you is that nobody can develop an unlimited network of close friends. But each of us needs about 20 friends who really know us and remain unconditional in their respect for us. We need to keep up-to-date in these friendships. Dr. E. Mansell Pattison describes the characteristics of healthy network friends:

1. There is frequent contact—weekly is best, and face-to-face is better than by letter or phone.

2. There is a positive emotion at every contact. You feel suddenly better and healthier, and you break into a smile on sight. Dr. Pattison makes the point that we do not keep people in our networks if they are doing negative things to themselves or to us. It takes too much energy. We may have been "stuck" during childhood, but we can choose healthy support relationships now that we are becoming adults. Healthy people do not violate, humiliate or berate

family members who have abused them. But healthy folks don't continue to "dance the dance" of abuse either.

3. There is a risk that the relationship might cost you something. You might have to interrupt your life to help the person in an emergency.

4. The risk is mutual. You know that the people in your network would interrupt their lives to help you in an emergency.

Look what you have if you intentionally create and maintain a healthy network. If you suffered from verbal or physical abuse as a child, if you were abandoned by a parent or if you felt exploited and misunderstood when you were a helpless child whose freedom was very limited, you can now celebrate! You can create a network of respect and affirmation, and be "reparented." You can create a "new family" of support and encouragement. And you can give as much as you receive. Health and healing will flourish as we all get into these intentional networks.

SEDUCTION INTO SEX

Ron spent summers and after school playing in his neighborhood during his elementary school years. The kids were in and out of each other's houses. Many had two working parents, so raiding the refrigerator for soda and snacks was common. Betty, who lived next door to Ron, told him a secret on one of these refreshment runs: her Dad had sex videos hidden, but she knew where he kept them. Would Ron like to watch one? Nobody was home, and her parents' schedule was perfectly predictable.

So the video rolled. These weren't "late night movies," but plain porno films. Ron told me he and Betty had these secret meetings from age nine until he was 12, and that they tried reenacting almost everything they saw on the videos.

"Finally, I knew this was terrible stuff, and I stopped. I had grown up a lot," Ron said, "and besides—I knew I could now make Betty pregnant. So I just stopped cold. But those pictures keep rolling in my head, and what I did with Betty is so vivid in my memory that I just can't get it out of my mind. I have trouble looking at any girl at school without seeing myself trying all of those things with her. And I masturbate several times a day, just going crazy with the stuff in my head."

SANCTIFYING SEXUAL ENERGY

Ron had also told me, "I feel like dead meat. Everything is literally screwed up, turned around. Can I ever think straight again?"

Most boys would have given in to watching sex videos, I told Ron. And the effects would have been devastating on anyone whose sexual awakening and sexual experience were triggered by pornography or seduction of any kind. When your body is the "sex victim," you can count the cost easily.

1. You begin to lose your sense of self-worth and think instead of your "sex worth." How much pleasure can you get, how soon, how often? What strategies do you use to get the most, quickest, and with new dimensions?

2. As you become preoccupied with sex and fun, you start seeing other people as "meat." They become "objects" to you, either in fantasy or in a widening circle of experimenting with "using people."

3. The danger isn't that a person masturbates occasionally, but that preoccupation with "pleasuring yourself" can make you a "user" addict—a person who uses people for his own pleasure, then disposes of them before it costs him anything permanent. The addict feels ashamed when an episode is over, whether it is masturbation or sex with

someone else. He feels "less of a person" than before. But after a few hours or days or weeks, his desire awakens. He slips into a sort of hypnotic trance and begins the ritual that normally delivers the episode of pleasure. Then he hits shame again and the cycle is complete. The addict's cycle goes round and round as he digs himself a black hole of shame.

RECOVERING FROM SEXUAL ADDICTION

Sex addicts, by this definition, require healing for self-respect. Like Dan with his hard family life, they will otherwise slip into the black hole of self-hatred. They will feel like dirt. Those are "shame" feelings. Shame feels ashamed, dirty, incompetent. Shame makes you feel much worse than a zero. You actually feel like you are a fraud: *If people knew what kind of a rotten jerk I really am, they wouldn't want anything to do with me.*

So healing from compulsive or abusive sexual behavior requires outside help—the mentor, to whom you can reveal the worst about yourself, then the support network I outlined in Dan's case earlier in this chapter.

But the "sexaholic" requires special help—healing of core ideas about yourself and your sexual energy. In some ways the sexaholic is like the foodaholic. We are glad that alcoholics can "swear off" alcohol and not touch it for the rest of their lives. But some addicts can't simply swear off. If foodaholics abstained, they would soon starve. In the same way, sexaholics must continue to be sexual persons, must deal with sexual thoughts and issues and must tend to their reproductive energy day by day. What the sexual addict must find is a way to *transform* or change sexual ideas and practices. Here are some strategies that work:

1. Get serious about understanding sex. A good place

to begin is chapter 9: "Take Your Curiosity to the Bible." If you have a research interest, don't be afraid to read the technical journals and research books about human sexuality. If your pastor or other respected mentor can be trusted with your curiosity, ask him to lend you the best books he has or tell you where to look. Male sexual energy is so powerful that you simply cannot abstain from thinking about sex. You may succeed for a few weeks, but "denial" soon explodes from underground, and your compulsive sexual behavior is likely to set a world record that drives you deeper into your shame pit. So get good, honest and technically accurate information. You will find more from me on this subject in my books *Bonding: Relationship in the Image of God; Re-Bonding: Preventing and Restoring Damaged Relationships; Lovers: Whatever Happened to Eden?* and *Parents, Kids, and Sexual Integrity*.

2. Focus your imagination on *what you really want*. Sexual imagination is controllable—like making your own videos. If some compulsive sex image strikes you, quickly be ready with some "videotape vision" of your sexual future *you want it to be*. If you fill that video with explicit images of your "exclusive, lifelong intimate knowing" of a partner, then you are rehearsing fidelity, monogamy and intimacy as you think sexually. When some inappropriate image appears, you can quickly "transform" the person or people involved into imagining *their* best future in exclusive, lifelong, intimate bonding in their own marriages.

Since male sexual energy is so persistent, as I described for you in chapter 7, you are facing a lifetime discipline job. But, as all of us know, wonderful possibilities are always showing up alongside terrible potential risks. So accept the challenge of surrendering your sexual energy to God and accepting *sanctifying grace* day by day to keep you on the track of fulfilling your best dreams.

Christ's love covers *all* our failures—remember that! And don't worry about dreams that occur when you are in deep sleep. Thankfully, most of these we do not remember! But dreams that are interrupted by your awaking are often remembered. Remember that most of what you dream is "garbage" that your deep consciousness is disposing of. So let the stuff go. People who have been deeply hurt or in painful family stress often have nightmares. Sometimes they are violent and frightening. But the "garbage disposal" view of those dreams helps them to "let go" of the junk that is being nicely disposed of during sleep. So a garbage dream episode might just be a good piece of housecleaning.

Maybe you're saying, "Okay that's good news, but it makes me feel like dirt because I made a big mistake." You may be holding in a stupid sex secret—of any kind. Maybe you went to bed with a girl, or experimented masturbating with another guy. Maybe some experienced person talked you into something that violated the best gift you've got. So you wail, "What can I do? Can I ever feel good about myself?"

The answer is the biggest "Yes!" in the world. God who has created every person "GOOD" can make you "NEW" through Jesus. The way to becoming new is to tell the whole mess to Jesus and accept His forgiveness. The "dirt" feeling can turn into "godly sorrow" and that is a sign of true repentance—turning away from ever going back again to that kind of stupid use of sex.

You are clean again and ready to take up your sexual gift and get it ready for one exclusive woman God will help you find. She has to be somebody to whom you can tell all of your secrets, so let Jesus seal off all of your past failures and get ready to look into the eyes of a woman who will love you with all of your childhood and all of your secrets.

CAUGHT IN THE ADULT CROSS FIRE

Bob told me he felt like a yo-yo. He was lucky to be in a picture-perfect family: parents and two kids, a boy oldest, then a girl. They were super religious. I first met Bob when he was 13 and was flunking all subjects in middle school. His mother arranged the consultation. I explained the ground rules to both Bob and his mother: I would work with Bob with the understanding that we were working on his school problems. Anything he needed to talk with me about would be between us, and I would advise his mother if we needed help from home.

At the same time, Bob was into high voltage religious experience at church, and into drugs at school. I recognized immediately that some strange "motor" must be driving both of these patterns. It wasn't hard to find. Mom and Dad were at each other's throats about everything, but especially about child-rearing policies. Dad was laid-back, and figured the kids would make it. After all, *he* had. Mom was determined to do it right. She also bought into the idea that Bob's dad was the head of the house, so she made it her business to get Dad busy doing his business, which was actually *her* business of running the kids *her* way. He couldn't do it with a clear conscience, so he escaped to work and put in a lot of overtime selling cars.

It was Mom who was stuck with managing the kids. Her temper flashed with punishment, guilt and shame from wall-to-wall. For example, Bob was not permitted to carry money, even what he earned working at Hardee's after school. His money was "in the bank." His mom had seen to it that he could not make a withdrawal without parental signature. So he started cheating, keeping money back without their knowledge. Then he was stuck, because there was no privacy at all in the house, and if he bought something he really wanted he couldn't take it home or they would know he had either stolen it or stowed some money somewhere.

Bob was caught as the oldest kid in a "Competitive Family" that was working hard at being a "Showcase Family." I described four kinds of families in chapter 3, and there are complete descriptions in my book, *Parents, Kids, and Sexual Integrity.* Because of the conflict between Bob's mom and dad, I describe him as caught in the cross fire. Sometimes he feels like a pawn—used, sacrificed— by his mom or his dad or both. And when the lightning strikes between his parents, or when he is the victim of his mother's rage or his father's workaholism as he avoids conflict, Bob tenses. His breathing pattern changes. His belly tightens. His digestion freezes or goes into diarrhea. He feels like either fighting to protect himself or running away to avoid the craziness going on.

What I have described in Bob's family is a "Stressor Family." There is a dominant stress maker, usually Mom. Everybody knows that when she is around, you walk on tiptoe. You hide your own needs and feelings, because Mom has moved in like a snowplow, and her agenda is the only agenda. Other members of such families, sometimes called "codependents," are caught in a "dance" over which they have almost no control. Often these dancers never get their needs met, and are unable to look to their families for support and comfort. They are easy victims of compulsive, almost unexplainable, exaggerated emotions and behavior.

The "stressor" may be any member of the family. That person may suffer a serious or terminal illness, which demands everybody's first attention. Or it may be an imagined or fake illness. It may be a food addiction, workaholism, alcoholism, a rage addiction, gambling or sexual promiscuity. It may be addiction to religion, community volunteering or any emotional or humanitarian compulsion—that makes the family "pay the rent" for the endless hours the stressor invests. In the process family members are abandoned and abused.

ESCAPING CRAZY-MAKING

Codependency can really mess up things. How do you break away from this dance of deformity? How do you discover who you might really be if you were taken seriously, valued and nurtured into responsible manhood?

Here again the help is outside the family. The rule is simple: Find health somewhere else and get yourself emotionally adopted into a set of relationships where everybody counts and everybody is valued and respected. You can find families like this if you will connect up with the church, scouts or community recreation, and if you will keep your eyes and ears open at school and in the community. You are smart enough, if you are in a crazy-making, stressor home, to spot dangerous people in anybody's house. Here are some tips for locating a healthy family:

1. Listen to how their kids talk about each parent. Ask questions about how they get along with each parent.

2. Listen to how these friends of yours talk about brothers and sisters. Is there an instinct to protect each other?

3. Get yourself invited to stay overnight or do a day trip with the family you admire. Seeing families interact over a period of 24 hours or more is like looking through a microscope—the real folks start coming out under normal family pressures.

4. If you can't locate a family with kids your age, open up your deep hunger and needs with a mentor, and accept invitations to join his younger family, to be the kid he and his wife never had or the replacement for the one who grew up and is now out on his own. Follow the mentor suggestions from earlier in this chapter.

5. Avoid like the plague hooking up with a mentor or a surrogate mom or dad who treats primary family relationships shabbily. Anybody who "cancels his family" to be your "caregiver" is only inviting you into a sick codependency, and you don't need more of that.

You are rebuilding a sense of your own worth, so pay attention to the networking and truth telling I laid down, too.

THE BOTTOM LINE

It's as simple as this. If you can name your pain, you can be healed of it. In the stories of Dan, Ron and Bob, I have wanted to open the basic doors through which most hurting young men may need to walk.

God, who made all things whole, complete and "good," can make you new again. Jesus is the advertising, the pointer; His abuse, death and resurrection are the "rent" paid to transform you in this present life.

And I am for you. As long as I live, I will keep an open line for you at 606-858-3817. Or you can write a letter to me and mail it to the publisher whose address is in the front of this book. I'll help you locate the support you need—somewhere in your community, very likely. Get your encouragement from any safe person near you, of course, but know that nothing that has happened *to* you needs to *control* you.

CHAPTER NINE

TAKE YOUR CURIOSITY TO THE BIBLE

WHEN I was in the eighth grade, Jim Deaver, Ed Zortman, Lyman Dewell and I used every spare minute trekking to the back of the classroom to consult the *Webster's Unabridged Dictionary*. Bruce Ramsay, our teacher and the principal of the Fowler Elementary School, thought we were energetic and bright boys. Actually, Jason, we were often searching for technical terms about human sexuality. We were learning, by the not-so-innocent age of 13, a lot of *non*technical sexual words, but we suspected that if we could find them, there were powerful, plain English words that were not violent and obscene. We had a little luck, and found our vocabularies growing. We didn't pronounce all of the words accurately, since the silent dictionary wasn't much help to farm boys.

I was lucky in my search for understanding the meaning of being human and sexual, since my search also went with me to church. I was inducted at about 13 into the youth group, where Ruth Crown quickly took my piano lesson skills and turned them into reading voice parts on any song in the world.

The young men at church were even more interested in finding out about being male and being sexual. We discovered sex in the Bible—a lot of it. My Uncle George taught us to use the concordance in our Bibles during excellent years in Sunday School. So if the sermon occasionally missed real life, there was always the concordance at the back of the Oxford *King James Version* of the Bible I had bought with my own money when I was about 11 years old. I still throw that badly worn Bible into my briefcase if I am flying out and need to track down some biblical resources. It is marked and worn out, but I can even remember exactly where on the page any favorite passage lies—what it looks like. I will likely turn to that old Bible as I put this chapter together, since I know that Bible best, remembering exact locations on pages where my favorite words appear. Its concordance is still better than some in so-called "study Bibles."

So in this chapter I am going to offer you a walking tour of the Old and New Testaments. Sometimes I will suggest a specific version to check out, but most of the time any Bible version or translation will get you to the right stuff.

What I predict is this: *You are going to find, as I did then and as I do now, that the Bible is powerfully positive about your identity, and about human sexuality in particular.* If you find a "sex-negative" statement, look carefully. I have never found a sex-negative Bible statement that was not protecting the crown jewels of human life—personal identity and relationships. I'm inviting you to fasten your seat belt and get ready for *a sex-positive tour of Holy Scripture.*

CREATION AND THE "IMAGE OF GOD"

You are a worthwhile person. In fact, you are at the peak of God's creation work. In sequence, humans appeared last on this planet. But in responsibility, humans are fixed at the center—responsible for themselves and for the careful management of all animals, birds, reptiles and the earth itself.

The Bible view of you is that you are the best there is: "Very good!" God said. This means, "I can't improve on this species, or create one any more complete, competent and full of potential for everything needed on planet Earth."

And the Bible picture of you is that you are "created in the image of God." Which is to say that since God is creative, so are you. Since God is just, you instinctively cry

The Bible is powerfully positive about your identity, and about human sexuality in particular.

out, "No fair!" when you are cheated, and you step in to interfere when somebody else is violated. God's image stamped into your genes means you are uniquely self-conscious, reflective and imaginative. All of the things God is, you are created to reflect.

Now for the sexual part. By some fantastic mystery, God's image in you, the Bible teaches, is expressed in your male sexual energy, identity and everything masculine about you! Let me take the masculine generic pronouns out, using my own translation of Genesis 1:27, "So God created the Adam in God's own image. In the image of God, the Adam was created. Male and female, God created them—from the Adam." You can read almost exactly the same summary in Genesis 5:1-2, where the *New International Version* of the Bible speaks of Adam in the same way. Check the footnote to see that "man" is actually "Adam." So when they were created, he called them "Adam." Look at the exact sequence of the statement about the man and the woman being created in God's "image." There is something about your being male and masculine that uniquely represents something about

God—just as there is something unique about a woman's ability to represent God.

I suspect this "image of God male and female" design means we need to keep a sex-balance everywhere: in marriage, in family, in organizations, in the church—in all of our systems and structures. If God depends on men and women to carry unique parts of the image of God, then we surely don't want to make big decisions without getting both male and female perspectives.

The most amazing sexual mystery is this: God evidently was most happy about how much fun it was to create human beings. If so, we can understand that God's gift of sexuality equips *us* to be creators, too. It takes one adult man and one adult woman to make a baby. We can create more humans! But we are not like some of the species in which one parent can make a baby and take good care of it. The infant dependent period for humans is so long—about 15 years!

Every human baby needs both sides of God's caring "image" to shape it into a healthy adult male or female over at least that long a span of years. Besides having a long childhood, humans need very complicated parenting, requiring specific things that fathers do better than mothers and others that mothers do better than fathers. So every baby deserves to have a father and a mother: both sides of that amazing "image of God." And you can look back at chapter 8 to review the kinds of tough stuff any kid may have to deal with if that ideal "image bearer" arrangement has been damaged or destroyed.

I also realize that many young men today are being raised by only one parent. Perhaps you come from a single-parent home. Remember that with your parent's help and love, along with a strong mentor and network of friends, you can come through with flying colors.

Now, hang on! Being created "in the image of God" seems also to mean that it's "godly" for males and females to long for each other! Get this: the mystery of the Trinity means that God, Christ and the Holy Spirit live in perfect community with each other. Furthermore, Jesus' prayer in John 17:20-23 shows that he yearns to bring *us* into the kind of unity the Trinity enjoys. The Old Testament illustrates this by speaking of God as the "Husband" and Israel as His "Bride." And in the New Testament Jesus is the "Groom" and "Head," while believers—the Church—are the "Bride" and the "Body." All this leads to a fascinating question: *Is God's "image" reflected in the way we yearn for each other sexually?*

This intimate language also tells us that our need to be united with God's purposes and character, to be holy and fired with justice and compassion, is so deep that God uses almost explicit sexual images to remind us of our need to join purposes with God. Our deep, ongoing need to become one with that "other self"—and our need for a lifelong commitment to her—are God's image in us. But these human, physical yearnings may also be God's way of hooking us—reminding us that human intimacy is only rehearsal for the ultimate intimacy we are working on: intimacy with God.

You can read about the image of God, male and female, in Genesis 1:26-28. Adam was "split" in Genesis 2 into the first man, Ish and the first woman, Ishah. The man turned against the woman, dominating her and renaming her "Eve." (To read more about this, follow the text and center column words in the *New American Standard Bible* or footnote "g" early in chapter 5 of Genesis in some editions of the *New International Version*. If you get a copy of *Lovers: What Ever Happened to Eden?* which my wife Robbie and I wrote to unravel this image of God, male and female issue, we will walk you through all of these images in slow motion.

MAN AND WOMAN AS "ONE FLESH, NAKED AND UNASHAMED"!

You can see that Adam in Genesis 1 is plural—humankind! "Male and female he created *them.*" Then, Genesis 2 describes how this complete Adam is actually divided to create woman, then man. I sometimes refer to this as "God's first splitting of the Adam!" The text tells us that God created Adam from *a-dam-ah*—a Hebrew word describing the dust particles of the earth that became the raw materials for "Adam."

When Adam is split into female and male parts of God's image, God is portrayed as a surgeon. Adam's thoracic cavity or rib cage is laid wide open. That cage has ribs (Hebrew *tsela*), so a boat construction word is used. Human ribs, like the ribs of a wooden hull of a boat, support the outer "skin" or covering. When Genesis was translated into the first Greek Bible, the translators called the ribs *pleura*, denoting the cavity where you may have felt sharp pains we still call "pleurisy," shooting around the entire rib cage.

With this complete Adam laid wide open, God built up the woman from those parts taken from the thoracic cavity, closing up the remains. "These better parts," we say, "were formed into woman—the feelings, the tenderness for people, the ability to speak her feelings were given to her." You have likely heard your dad or grandpa refer to your mom or grandma as "My better half!" But the leftover part of Adam was the male.

The surgical picture is used to tell us three things:

1. Both male and female are made from Adam, and they are created as temples of the "breath of God" or the Holy Spirit and as bearers of God's image.

2. Sex differences are profound. Women are super-built for attachment and concern for relationships. Men are under-equipped for expressing feelings, but super-built with muscle, strength and the ability to zero in on urgent tasks that have to be done in spite of feelings.

3. Either is incomplete without the other. They were formed first as one; when separate they are alone and need missing dimensions they cannot always identify. The loneliness in the solitary male or female is often felt as a cosmic loneliness. It is not specifically sexual loneliness, but people who run with only their own gender tend to be trying to clap with one hand in a universe that is calling them to a standing ovation.

Back to our story. Upon recovery from their surgery, Ish and Ishah are magnetically attracted to each other. "Wow!" the male says, "this is bone of my bone and flesh of my flesh! This shall be called Ishah, for she was formed out of Ish!" So there in the presence of God and without a priest, preacher or rabbi, the whole universe cried out: "Because of how they are created, Ish shall magnetically bond to Isahah and they shall become one intimate flesh, naked and without shame!" Much later, trying to get us back to this wonderful picture of "the way it is supposed to be," Jesus added another wonderful line recorded for all time in Matthew 19: 4-6: "What therefore God has glued together let no one anywhere, anytime, on earth break apart!" (This is my loose, but faithful, conceptual translation.)

I suggest you work slowly through Genesis 2 in two or three translations and review our unraveling of it in *Lovers: What Ever Happened to Eden*? You can read Jesus' words about the "epoxy glue" bond in Matthew 19, where He is frowning on people who trivialize marriage and who recommend divorce for a thousand irrelevant reasons.

INTIMATE "KNOWING": INTERCOURSE, CONCEPTION AND BIRTH

I was baffled when I was young because of the way the Old Testament talks about couples and how they get a baby. After a conception, the Bible would read, over and over again: "Adam knew Eve his wife, and she conceived...," "Cain knew his wife, and she conceived...," "Elkanah knew Hannah his wife...." And when Mary and Joseph discovered she was pregnant with the special conception that gave us Jesus, the Son of God, the text reports, "Joseph knew her not, until she had borne a son." You can see this strange language of the old *King James Version* if you look at Genesis 4:1, 17, 25; 1 Samuel 1:19 and Matthew 1:25. Newer translations are more clearly sexual. Joseph, for example, "had no union with" Mary until she had delivered her son, according to the *New International Version.*

The Hebrew word translated "know" or "knew" suggests *real* knowing—stripping away masks and secrets. In a healthy bonded marriage, when two people have voluntarily shared their vision and their secrets they are certainly on the way to "knowing" each other. So the Hebrew idea suggests that an enduring, lifelong relationship requires "getting to know" each other, and guarantees intimate joining, union and the literal merging of the two.

THE TABOOS: ADULTERY, FORNICATION AND RAPE

In the Bible there are a few cases where "knowing" is used in the sense of ripping away the secrets and violating a person. One tragic example of this kind of "knowing" appears in Judges 19:25. A man's concubine left him, and was practicing prostitution or at least sleeping around with other men back in her hometown. So he went after her to bring her back. On their return they stopped in the city of Gibeah and prepared to spend the night on the street. But an old man urged them,

> "Let me supply whatever you need. Only don't spend the night in the square." So he took him into his house and fed his donkeys. After they had washed their feet, they had something to eat and drink.
>
> While they were enjoying themselves, some of the wicked men of the city surrounded the house. Pounding on the door, they shouted to the old man who owned the house, "Bring out the man who came to your house so we can have sex with him."
>
> The owner of the house went outside and said to them, "No, my friends, don't be so vile. Since this man is my guest, don't do this disgraceful thing. Look, here is my virgin daughter, and his concubine. I will bring them out to you now, and you can use them and do to them whatever you wish. But to this man, don't do such a disgraceful thing."
>
> But the men would not listen to him. So the man took his concubine and sent her outside to them, and they raped her and abused her throughout the night, and at dawn they let her go. At daybreak the woman went back to the house where her master was staying, fell down at the door and lay there until daylight.

You can read the whole horror story in Judges 19. I have quoted verses 20-26 from the *New International Version.*

When the man found his concubine unconscious on the doorstep the next morning, the man put her on his donkey and took her home. What he did next may have been a parable or merely a deeper sign of his own wickedness. He cut her into 12 parts and distributed her body into all 12 tribal areas of Israel. So the story provoked people to cry out everywhere: "Such a thing has never been seen or done, not since the day the Israelites came up out of Egypt. Think about it! Consider it! Tell us what to do!" (v. 30).

The whole story describes the worst end of the range of things men are capable of doing to women. Since the tragedy of the first sin, recorded in Genesis 3, men have had a tendency to regard women as their property and to control them. *That is not God's design or God's will, and men who use women are always under God's judgment.* This story about violent "knowing" is as bad as it gets.

There are other words of illegal and inappropriate sexual contact. The heat of sexual desire sometimes drives people over the edge, with a sort of simple animal passion. "Lie with me" is a *King James* translation of the use of sexual passion purely for selfish gratification. Joseph, trusted by the Egyptian executive Potiphar, as an employee in his house, was propositioned for sex by Potiphar's wife. She "caught him by his garment, saying, 'Lie with me.'" The word for this sexual passion was very much like our use of the phrase, "go to bed," when it means simply "I want your sex, not lifelong responsibility and care for you." You can read this story in Genesis 39. Nothing much has changed about being "at risk" for sexual seduction and entrapment even today.

A third word in the Old Testament was used to describe sexual seduction. It was a violent term meaning the same as "rape." One of the most tragic stories in the Bible is of the rape of Tamar by her half brother Amnon. You can read the story in 2 Samuel 13. Amnon devised a plot to trick Tamar, pretending he was sick. Then he begged her to "lie with him," the seductive ploy for getting sex. When she agreed to marry him, but not to play around with him, he forced her; he "raped" her. Date rape, acquaintance rape and violent rape by a stranger are similar to Amnon's sin against Tamar. You can read the text and see the humiliation Tamar felt, and the vengeance her full brother, Absalom, planned against Amnon. It is easy to see that everything goes wrong when anyone is obsessed with getting sex without responsibility and respect for themselves and the other persons.

If you want to work through a terrifying chapter of warnings, most of them calling for the death penalty, look at Deuteronomy 22. When I first read it, I thought it was about "premarital sex,"—sex before marriage. But as I studied it, it became clear that this is not about premature bonding, but about one person "using" another sexually. And when you look at how emotionally damaged people are who use other people or get used by them, you may understand a primitive society that said simply, "Kill them!" They had no rehabilitation programs or psychiatrists. And they didn't have Jesus hanging on a cross and rising from the dead to establish a way to be "made new" again. So, damaged people were like broken-legged race horses. They simply had to be killed.

SONG OF SOLOMON: IMAGES OF SEXUAL LOVING

The classic love song of all time is in the Bible book called Song of Songs or Song of Solomon. Theologians have squeezed the book to try to extract spiritual messages, but it can be read simply as a book about sexual intimacy. What we have to remember, however, is that sexual intimacy, even holy sexual passion for an exclusive, lifelong partner, is the best human picture of powerful faith in God. And when we want to talk about our faith in God, we borrow words from marriage. The words "faithfulness" and "fidelity," for example, create images of sexual faithfulness and exclusive marital fidelity. If you want to sample the Song of Songs, try reading chapters 2, 4 and 5. You will see in 2:6 the description of the posture for sexual intimacy. Most of chapter 4 describes the yearning of the man for the woman, and most of chapter 5 describes the yearning of the woman for the man. Evidently the "garden" and the "fountain" references are to the intimate genital gifts they presented to each other.

JESUS: ULTIMATE RESPECT FOR HUMAN SEXUALITY

If you want to see the highest respect for human sexuality and marriage, read it in the words and actions of Jesus. He says, "What God joins together sexually, be careful not to rip apart!" Jesus announces the warning in the face of easy divorce in His teaching recorded in Matthew 19. He restates the Genesis 2 picture of one man and one woman forming one flesh unity, and suggests that the only alternative to the kind of beautiful sexual intimacy is holy celibacy: being single for the glory of God and the service of God's purposes in the world. It is clear that to be single and sexually unattached is an expression of high human responsibility and high respect for humans everywhere.

Jesus teaches responsible "looking" in the famous "lust" teaching in Matthew 5. We are to sanctify our sexual imagination and to be careful not to fantasize sexual intimacy with inappropriate people. This high target, which keeps all of us focused on our own lifelong intimacy covenant, means looking ahead toward marriage when we are young and looking back to reconstruct a lifelong fidelity for the rest of our lives. This sex-positive focusing of sexual imagination and energy is an invitation to clear and exclusive thinking as the highest respect we can show for everyone. We can imagine intimacy between married partners, the future marriage of our unmarried friends, and our own past and future with the exclusive woman of our magical choosing. No one has a higher, more positive view of sex then Jesus.

DIVORCE: UNSPEAKABLE LOSS AND PAIN

Jesus is more impatient with Jewish divorce practices than almost anything else. Read one of His sharp exchanges in Matthew 19 again. One group of Jewish leaders followed the school of Hillel, a leading rabbi. Hillel taught that Moses' law in Deuteronomy 24, about discovering "some naked thing" about your wife, meant "anything displeasing to you." So Jewish men, who were often polygamous, could dismiss wives for any trivial thing at all, much like firing a domestic employee. But the school of Shammai, another great rabbi, taught that only in case of some tragic exposure of past sexual disgrace could a man divorce his wife. So, in Matthew 19, the two groups got Jesus in the "cross fire" and wanted Him to take sides. Instead, He took them back to Genesis, to Creation, and gave them a kindergarten lesson in the meaning of marriage. He hit the crescendo with the warning: "Therefore what God has joined together, let [no one] separate"—a line you will hear recited at the end of every Christian wedding today.

But watch Jesus, in John 4, deal with a woman who had been married and divorced five times each, and who, in this shameful condition, was now living with a man to whom she was not married. Jesus clearly believes that divorce is not the end of hope. He puts her back on the track of abundant life. So Jesus is not simply a "purist" who shoots the wounded. He believes that anybody in any tragic condition can be salvaged and brought to wholeness and health today.

THE GHOST OF LOST LOVE

Jesus cautions about establishing a bond with a second woman after having bonded with one's first. His teaching is this: Remarriage after divorce [or a break up?] creates grief, and you may take a ghost to bed with your new partner. The rule seems to be that if you divorce, you violate a bond, but that bond is likely to survive and haunt the new marriage. This effect of mixing two bonds is called "adultery" or adulterated bonding. Only when the bond has been killed, mutilated by what Jesus calls "fornication" [also translated "harlotry" or "promiscuity"] can the victim remarry without carrying the ghost of the previous bond into—and adulterating—the new sexual relationship.

Read Jesus in Luke 16:18, for example: "Anyone who divorces his wife and marries another woman commits adultery, and the man who marries a divorced woman commits adultery." Now, notice that in Mark 10:11-12 Jesus raises the same warning to both the man and the woman: "Anyone who divorces his wife and marries another woman commits adultery against her. And if she divorces her husband and marries another man, she commits adultery." Matthew 5:32 and 19:9 add one exception, which if it is present, keeps the "adultery" ghost from appearing: anyone who divorces a spouse gets into adultery when they remarry—except when the divorce was a result of fornication/harlotry/promiscuity.

If you think, *Well I'm not married, so this doesn't apply to me,* think again. If powerful, intimate bonding "lives" to haunt the future, it will be important to avoid moving beyond bonding Step 6 until you can slowly move toward Steps 7-8-9 in a realistic and responsible sequence ready for a wedding at a fixed calendar date. Remember Step 6

The rule is this: Christians are people who remember their own weaknesses and failure. They are under reconstruction. So they offer hope and forgiveness to people who fail and who need Jesus' healing grace and hope.

hits "rotation" with Step 7. And a broken bond, even as early as Step 7, 8 or 9 can leave the ghost of a lost love. It is just like Jesus to caution about what one person can do to another. So a rebellious or hard-hearted person can break a relationship or a marriage, but the responsibility falls on that person for "causing the abandoned spouse" to commit adultery by taking a broken heart into another marriage. The victim of abandonment or divorce can take notice, too, that healing time, grief time and slow recovery are essential if they are to enter a new relationship without the ghost haunting their future.

The guidelines here apply equally to "breaking up" when dating. It is important to pay attention to feelings and attachment, and not to jump into a new dating relationship when grief is still heavy from the lost friendship. Otherwise, we mix bonds even though they are at very early stages and are far from becoming sexual. The principle of healing before starting over applies to all of us for a lifetime.

TRANSFORMATION OF FAILURE AND LOSS

I pointed you to the famous "woman at the well" story in John 4 to illustrate how Jesus accepted and gave hope to people who had suffered multiple marriages and divorces, and how He helped her to begin again from where she was. Since women were more likely to be the victims of sexual abuse and divorce in Jesus' day, the clearest examples of His care and affirmation are for such women. In Luke 7:36-50, for example, a "woman who had lived a sinful life" invades a dinner party to bathe Jesus' feet with perfumed water. Jesus takes the occasion to announce her forgiveness and to rebuke the host, who wanted to throw the woman out.

In the opening verses of John 8, a woman who has been "caught in the act of adultery" is dragged to Jesus by Jewish men who want to test Jesus by asking Him to pronounce judgment on her. Jesus surprises the men by announcing that only those "without sin" will be permitted to throw stones to execute her. So, again, Jesus is "for" the victims and "against" the proud people with good reputations.

The apostle Paul reminds the early Christians in Colossians 3:2-15, to remember their own broken past lives:

> Set your minds on things above, not on earthly things. For you died, and your life is now hidden with Christ in God....Put to death, therefore, whatever belongs to your earthly nature: sexual immorality [fornication], impurity, lust, evil desires and greed, which is idolatry....You used to walk in these ways, in the life you once lived. But now you must rid yourselves of all such things as these: anger, rage, malice, slander, and filthy language from your lips. Do not lie to each other, since you

have taken off your old self with its practices and
have put on the new self, which is being renewed
in knowledge in the image of its Creator....Bear
with each other and forgive whatever grievances
you may have against one another....Let the peace
of Christ rule in your hearts."

The rule is clear: Christians are people who remember
their own weakness and failure. They are under reconstruc-
tion. So they offer hope and forgiveness to people who
fail and who need Jesus' healing grace and hope.

BRIDES, GROOMS, WEDDINGS AND INTIMACY

When the Bible wants to make its highest and best point, it
does so with stories and word pictures of exclusive man-
woman relationships that lead to public celebration and
sexual intimacy. So, the creation of humans is the peak of
the Genesis Creation story, and the detailed version of the
human creation in chapter 2 has the man and woman both
formed "bone" and "flesh" from the same Adam. But the
plot hits the heavens when the new couple turn out to be
spellbound with discovering each other, falling into each
other's arms and reuniting the "one flesh"!

So a man and a woman, to this day, enter the best of all
possible worlds when they turn away from home and parents and form a new unity, naked and without shame—
"one flesh." Together they will, if things go right, form "one
flesh" babies who themselves will become women and
men in due time. These "bone of my bone, flesh of my
flesh" children, will then find and form other primary
bonds. That story is as good as it gets.

And when God wants to picture the relationship with
humans, He is the Husband married to Israel, and Jesus is
married to the Church. Neither is a "perfect marriage," just

as no human marriage is perfect. But God joins with humans to form an eternal, exclusive bond. We are "born into" God's kingdom. We are suckled and nurtured by Mother Church. We may even carry on adolescent "love-hate" battles with Mother Church and with Father God, but we always yearn to "come home" to Jesus, to the Father and to the Church. If we return, it will be with honest repentance and visible eagerness for the reunion.

The ultimate homecoming will also be a wedding. You can read about it in Revelation 19 and 21. Notice in Revelation 18:21-24 the list of things that will never be heard in the evil city, Babylon, again. Among those missing sounds is this: "The voice of bridegroom and bride will never be heard in you again." Weddings are celebrations. Some, unfortunately, may have been preceded by premature intimacy, even "living together." But weddings are public, community peak experiences; and where evil spreads, celebrations fade away. Look at how the celebration of the ages is described in Revelation 19:7, where the wedding/marriage of the Lamb (Jesus) and His bride (the Church) has come. Notice how the bride is dressed. Notice that those are truly blessed who get an invitation to "the wedding supper" of Jesus and the Church.

Now, jump to Revelation 21 and read from the top. In contrast to Babylon, the evil city, here is Jerusalem, the Holy City—the residence of the true believers, the Church eternal. She is "coming down out of heaven from God, prepared as a bride beautifully dressed for her husband." The best news ever announced is this: from this time on God is present, living among the people. As verses 3-4 say, "They will be his people, and God himself will be with them and be their God. He will wipe every tear from their eyes."

All of this final wedding celebration is taking place on the banks of the "river of the water of life, as clear as crystal, flowing from the throne of God and of the Lamb down the middle of the great street of the city." You can read this setting for the "wedding supper of the Lamb" in Revelation 22, which contains a final invitation in verse 17. Here it is with plural pronouns to make clear how wide the invitation is: "The Spirit [the Holy Spirit] and the bride say, 'Come!' And let [those] who hear say, 'Come!' Whoever is thirsty, let [them] come; and whoever wishes, let [them] take the free gift of the water of life."

Do you see the big picture, Jason? History begins with a solitary Adam, split into man and woman, who reunite as "one flesh, naked and without shame." And history will end with Jesus, who is called the Second Adam by Saint Paul. Jesus, too, was "split"— at the pleura, when the tip of a Roman soldier pierced His side and He hung on the cross. And Jesus' Bride was formed out of His opened side. We call her the Body of Christ, the Church. Although she has been separated from the Groom all these years, here in Revelation 22, at the end of time, the Bride is finally reunited with the Groom at the marriage supper of the Lamb. There both the Bride and the Groom turn out to be Jesus, the Second Adam, split, but being reunited for eternity. That happy wedding is one you and I are being invited to participate in.

In the meantime, your sexual energy and your yearning for intimacy are one of God's powerful ways of keeping your attention and your affection on the real Wedding. Make your human loving holy and pure, because it is your own personal rehearsal for the real thing, forever. Eternity is far longer than this lifetime. Get ready for the Big Wedding!

So there is the walking tour of the Bible on intimacy and sexuality. And this brings us to saying good-bye. This book was dedicated to you, Jason, Jordan and Justin—my special connections to the future.

While I was focusing with you on your future, these last months, you and I suddenly lost my dad—your great-grandfather. We were lucky to have him with us over the winter holidays while we were letting him go. Jason's self-appointed all-night vigil alone with Dad was a rite of passage into manhood, all in itself. But the multi-generation linkage was given its final forging when Dad saw you, Jason, standing by the bed. I asked him, "What do you think of the six-foot-tall young man standing there?"

He was suddenly bright and witty: "It looks like a young Marvin to me." His linkage to the future was clear and peaceable.

Then, at Betts and West Funeral Home when our tribe had its own time alone to honor Dad, I noticed you, Justin and Jordan, reaching over into the casket. I wondered what you were doing. But then, I myself had straightened his tie. He held a rosebud with baby's breath in his hands—the symbol of a new great-granddaughter born in England a week before. On the way to dinner, you guys told me what you had been doing.

"Grandpa," you said, "we looked until we found coins with all of our birth years on them and we stuck them in Granddaddy's pockets. How long will it be till they rot?"

Wow! I thought, *these guys are not only hooked into their own manhood and their own future, they are determined to go into his future.*

The real answer would have been, of course, "I don't know how long coins will last underground." But I cheated. I was so elated at your ingenious way of sending something of yourselves into the ground with Dad. I answered, almost exploding with pride in your fantastic idea, "In the resurrection, when Jesus calls him from the grave, he's going to be the only one there with money in his pockets—and they will be keepsakes from his six great grandchildren."

I'm glad I'm in your family. Thanks for being Joy men—
for hooking into what the family is about, and for taking
responsibility, literally, ahead of your time.